MANDU

His Highness Anandrao Puar
Maharaja of Dhār

MANDU

THE CITY OF JOY

By

G. YAZDANI, M.A.

GYAN

Published by

GYAN

Gyan Publishing House
5, Ansari Road
Daryaganj, New Delhi-110002
Phone: 011-47034999, 9811692060
E-mail: books@gyanbooks.com

Distribution Network
gyanbooks.com
India, USA, Canada, UK, Australia, France

ISBN : 978-81-212-6657-4 (PB)
First Published, 1929

2nd Impression 2022

Printed at: Gyan Press, Delhi.

MANDU: The City of Joy
Author: G. YAZDANI

MANDŪ

The City of Joy

BY

G. YAZDANI, M.A.

DIRECTOR OF ARCHAEOLOGY IN
H.E.H. THE NIZAM'S DOMINIONS
AND EPIGRAPHIST TO THE
GOVERNMENT OF INDIA FOR
MOSLEM INSCRIPTIONS

Lo, the owl hath built her nest
In Shirwan Shāh's high storey,
Warning nightly by her cry,
'Where now thy pomp and glory?'

AKBAR'S INSCRIPTION AT MANDŪ

1929

PREFACE

THE romantic history of Mandū and the tales of its beautiful monuments had always fascinated me and I often dreamt of visiting the Pleasure City (Shādīābād) where King Ghiyāth-ud-Dīn held a retinue of 15,000 damsels or where the gallant Chief, Bāz Bahādur, was allured by the sweet voice of Rūpmatī. The realization of my dreams, however, came in a somewhat unexpected manner.

His Highness the Maharaja of Dhār, in whose territory Mandū is situated, came to hear of my interest in archaeology and was kind enough to send me an assurance of welcome and an invitation to visit his State. His Exalted Highness the Nizam was graciously pleased to grant me permission to take advantage of this kind offer and to treat my stay at Mandū as time spent on duty. This was in 1925, but shortly afterwards the regrettable news of the illness and subsequent death of the Maharaja of Dhār was received, and thus I never had the privilege of seeing the Ruler who had invited me to Mandū and whose name is so honoured in Central India.

The Dhār Darbar, however, continued to evince interest in my visit, and when I went over there in March 1927, the Dīwan, Rao Bahādur K. Nadkar, was kind enough not only to arrange for the comfort of my party, but also to lend me the services of a draughtsman to draw the plans of the important buildings. In the end, the Dhār Darbar were also pleased to propose that the results of my studies should be published at their expense in the form of a guide-book. I have therefore to thank the Dhār Darbar most sincerely not only for their hospitality and courtesy, but also for the opportunity they have given me of publishing the results of my studies in their present form.

As to the scope of this book, I must explain that it has been written for the ordinary visitor and may therefore be found lacking in those details which can be incorporated only in monographs of greater bulk. No endeavour, however, has been spared to present to the reader a clear account of the monuments, and with this object a large number of photographs and architectural plans have been included in the book.

Among previous works on Mandū two deserve special notice. One of them is the learned article by Mr. (afterwards Sir) J. M. Campbell,[1] which deals most carefully with the Moslem history of Mandū and may be studied with advantage by all interested in the subject.[2] The other work is the *History of Mandū, the Ancient Capital of Malwa*, by 'a Bombay Subaltern'.[3] The author has given an extremely vivacious account of his journey to Mandū, in which place it is as difficult to forget him as to forget Washington Irving in the Alhambra.

Finally, I wish to pay a tribute to the work at Mandū of the Archaeological Department of the Government of India, to whose care and attention the preservation of the monuments is mainly due. I must add that the Darbar have spared no trouble or expense in carrying out the

[1] Published in the *Journal* of the Bombay Branch of the Royal Asiatic Society, vol. xix, pp. 154–201, for 1895–7.

[2] The translations of the inscriptions as given in this article are not very accurate, and for them I would refer the reader to the *Epigraphia Indo-Moslemica* for 1909–10 and 1911–12.

[3] Originally published in 1855 and reprinted in Bombay in 1875.

suggestions of the department for the clearance of jungle and the repairs of masonry.

Before concluding I must also express my indebtedness to Mr. John Johnson, the Printer of the Oxford University Press, for his willing assistance and expert advice in the printing of the book.

G. YAZDANI.

HYDERABAD, DECCAN,
1st May, 1928.

CONTENTS

PREFACE v

I. PHYSICAL ASPECTS AND TOPOGRAPHY . . 1–4

Situation and climate, p. 1; Flora and fauna, pp. 2–3; Route, pp. 3–4.

II. HISTORY 5–40

Legendary period, p. 5; Paramāras, p. 6; Musalman conquests, p. 7; Dilāwar Khān Ghorī, pp. 8–9; Hoshang Shāh, pp. 10–13; Muḥammad Shāh, p. 14; Maḥmūd Khaljī, pp. 15–19; Ghīyāth-ud-Dīn, pp. 20–22; Nāṣir-ud-Dīn, pp. 23–25; Maḥmūd II, pp. 26–27; Sulṭān Bahādur of Gujarat and Humāyūn, p. 28; Qādir Shāh and Sher Shāh, p. 29; Shujā' Khān, p. 30; Bāz Bahādur, pp. 31–32; Akbar, p. 33; Jahāngīr, pp. 34–37; Shāhjahān, p. 38; Aurangzeb, p. 39; Marathas and Anand Rāo Puār, p. 40.

III. MONUMENTS 41–124

'Ālamgīr Darwāzah, p. 41; Bhangī Darwāzah, p. 42; Delhi Darwāzah, pp. 43–44; Tomb of Hoshang, pp. 45–49; Jāmi' Masjid, pp. 50–55; Trīpoliya Gate, p. 56; Madrasah or Ashrafī Maḥall, p. 57; Tower of Victory, p. 58; Tomb of Maḥmūd Khaljī, pp. 59–60; Ṭawelī Maḥall, pp. 61–62; Jahāz Maḥall or the Ship Palace, pp. 63–67; Royal Palaces and the Champa Bāolī, pp. 68–69; Hindolā Maḥall, pp. 70–73; Dilāwar Khān's Mosque, p. 74; Nahār Jharokā, pp. 75–76; Hāthī Pol Gate, p. 77; Ujālā Bāolī, p. 78; Andherī Bāolī, p. 79; Gadā Shāh's Shop, p. 79; Gadā Shāh's House, p. 80; Sāgar Talāo, p. 81; Mosque of Malik Mughīth, pp. 82–85; the Caravan Sarāi, p. 86; Dā'ī Kī Chhoṭī Baihan Kā Maḥall, pp. 86–87; Sāgarī Tank, p. 88; Dā'ī Kā Maḥall, p. 88; Echo Point, p. 89; Jālī Maḥall (No. 1), p. 90; Rīwā Kund, p. 91; Bāz Bahādur's Palace, pp. 92–96; Rūpmatī's Pavilions, pp. 97–99; Hāthī Maḥall, pp. 100–101; Daryā Khān's Tomb, pp. 102–103; Tomb to the north of Daryā Khān's Mausoleum, pp. 104–105; La'l Maḥall or Lāl Bungalow, pp. 106–107; Chishtī Khān's Palace, pp. 108–109; Chhappan Maḥall, p. 110; Nīl Kanth Palace, pp. 111–114; Songarh, p. 115; Tārāpūr Gate, pp. 116–117; Bhagwanīya Darwāzah, p. 118; Jahāngīrpūr Darwāzah, p. 119; Sāt sau Sīrhī, p. 120; Rāmpol Darwāzah, p. 121; Lohānī Darwāzah, p. 121; Sāt Kothrī, p. 122; Jālī Maḥall (No. 2), p. 123; Conclusion, p. 124.

INDEX 125–31

ILLUSTRATIONS

Frontispiece. His Highness Anandrao Puar, Maharaja of Dhār

I. Delhi Darwāzah 42
II. Hoshang's Tomb: Plan 44
III. Hoshang's Tomb: General view . . . 46
IV. Hoshang's Tomb: Interior 48
V. Jāmi' Masjid: Basement (Plan) . . . 50
VI. Jāmi' Masjid: Plan 50
VII. Jāmi' Masjid: General view 52
VIII. Jāmi' Masjid: Prayer Hall (façade) . . 54
IX. Jāmi' Masjid: Prayer Hall 56
X. Jāmi' Masjid: Pulpit and the Miḥrāb . . 56
XI. Ashrafī Maḥall, or the Madrasah: Plan . . 58
XII. Ashrafī Maḥall 58
XIII. Tomb of Maḥmūd Khaljī: Plan . . . 60
XIV. Tomb of Maḥmūd Khaljī 62
XV. Jahāz Maḥall: Plan 64
XVI. Jahāz Maḥall: General view from south-east . 64
XVII. Jahāz Maḥall and the Munja Talāo . . 66
XVIII. Ruins of the Royal Palaces 68
XIX. Hindolā Maḥall: (*a*) Ground Plan; (*b*) Upper storey 70
XX. Hindolā Maḥall: View from south-east . . 70
XXI. Hindolā Maḥall: View from west . . . 72
XXII. Hindolā Maḥall: Interior 74
XXIII. Gadā Shāh's Shop (?) 76
XXIV. Gadā Shāh's House (?) 78
XXV. Wall-painting in Gadā Shāh's House . . 80
XXVI. Wall-painting in Gadā Shāh's House . . 80
XXVII. Sāgar Talāo 82
XXVIII. (*a*) Mosque of Dilāwar Khān: Plan; (*b*) Mosque of Malik Mughīth: Plan 84
XXIX. Mosque of Malik Mughīth: Exterior . . 84

XXX. Mosque of Malik Mughīth: Prayer Hall (façade) 86
XXXI. Dā'ī Ki Chhotī Baihan Ka Maḥall 88
XXXII. Dā'ī Ka Maḥall 90
XXXIII. Rīwā Kund and Bāz Bahādur's Palace . . 92
XXXIV. Rīwā Kund: View from north-east . . 92
XXXV. Bāz Bahādur's Palace: Plan 94
XXXVI. Bāz Bahādur's Palace: Northern Hall . . 94
XXXVII. Bāz Bahādur's Palace: Southern Apartments . 96
XXXVIII. Rūpmatī's Pavilions: View from west . . 98
XXXIX. Rūpmatī's Pavilions: View from north-east . 100
XL. Hāthī Maḥall 102
XLI. (*a*) Hāthī Maḥall: Plan; (*b*) Daryā Khān's Tomb: Plan 102
XLII. Daryā Khān's Tomb: View from north-west . 104
XLIII. Daryā Khān's Tomb 104
XLIV. Lāl Bungalow 106
XLV. Chishtī Khān's Palace 108
XLVI. Chhappan Maḥall 110
XLVII. Nīl Kanth or Shāh Budāgh Khān's Palace . 112
XLVIII. Tārāpūr Gate 116
XLIX. Jālī Maḥall: Interior 124
Map of Mandū Fort . . . . . . *at end*

CHAPTER I

Physical Aspects and Topography

FEW FORTS can boast of such a situation as Mandū. It stands at the top of an offshoot of the Vindhyan Range, rising 2,079 feet above the sea-level and separated from the main plateau of Malwa by a deep ravine, which is forested with magnificent trees. This romantic gorge, which is called *Kākra Koh* on account of its fantastic windings, encircles the Mandū hill on three sides and finally emerges into the Nimar plain, which lies 1,200 feet below the Fort on the south.[1] The top of the hill, excepting a few knolls, among which the spur of Songarh is prominent, is almost flat: it extends three to four miles from north to south and four to five miles from east to west, the area being over 12,000 English acres.[2]

The climate is mild and bracing, and after the rains the verdure presents a spectacle the grandeur of which it is difficult to depict. The emperor Jahāngīr was fascinated by the scenery of the place and he writes thus in his *Memoirs*: 'What words of mine can describe the beauty of the grass and of the wild flowers? They clothe each

[1] The reader can form an idea of the irregular contour of the hill from the Survey Map inserted at the end of the book.

[2] Sir J. M. Campbell writes: 'During the palmy days of the fifteenth century, of the 12,000 acres of the Mandū hill-top, 560 were fields, 370 were gardens, 200 were wells, 780 were lakes and ponds, 100 were bazaar roads, 1,500 were dwellings, 200 were rest-houses, 260 were baths, 470 were mosques, and 334 were palaces. These allotments crowded out the wild to a narrow pittance of 1,560 acres of knolls and ridges.' *J.B.R.A.S.*, vol. xix, p. 156.

hill and dale, each slope and plain. I know of no place so pleasant in climate and so pretty in scenery as Mandū in the rainy season. This month of July, which is one of the months of the hot season, the sun being in Leo, one cannot sleep within the house without a coverlet, and during the day there is no need for a fan. What I have noticed is but a small part of the many beauties of Mandū.'

The fair table-land is interspersed with many a lake and pool, the transparent waters of which reflect the rich foliage of mangoes, *khirnīs*, tamarinds, and banyans growing in abundance on their banks.[1] Mixed among these beautiful trees the visitor cannot fail to notice the unseemly baobab (*Adansonia digitata*) with its huge swollen trunk and leafless branches from which the fruits hang like pendent gourds.[2] The tree is in leaf only during the rains. Locally it is called the *Khurāsānī Imlī* and is supposed to have been introduced into Mandū from Africa during the reign of Maḥmūd Khaljī (1436–69), when Malwa had close trade relations with that continent. The French botanist, Adanson, who discovered the tree, believed that it exceeded any other in longevity. He noticed a tree the trunk of which was 30 feet in diameter, and calculated the age of it at 5,150 years.

The fauna of Mandū is equally interesting, and, although the tigers are now not so dominant as 'to carry off troopers riding in the ranks of their regiments',[3] yet

[2] Abul Faḍl has confused this tree with the tamarind (*Tamarindus indica*, Indian *Imlī*) and writes in the *Ā'īn*: 'Here the tamarind grows as large as a cocoanut and its kernel is extremely white.' Jarrett's translation, vol. ii, p. 197.

[3] Briggs's *Firishta* (English translation), vol. iv, p. 235 (footnote).

the lordly beast holds undisputed sway in the secluded dales of the Fort, and we often hear of transgressors, whether man or animal, having received condign punishment for their temerity. Panthers patrol the streets during the night, and the bear is a frequent prowler. Among the innocent denizens of the plateau a large variety of deer may be met, while the frolicsome monkey is to be seen everywhere, dancing and jumping from bough to bough and stopping anon to offer defiance to the intruder. In early summer the air resounds with the sweet notes of birds, some of which have magnificent plumage. The emperor Jahāngīr, during his stay, was much interested in the nest of the wagtail (*Mamola*), which is called *Dum-sīja* (tail-wagger) in Persian. He writes in his *Memoirs*: 'Up till now none of the hunters had pointed out its nest. By chance in the building I occupied there was its nest, and it had two young ones.'[1]

Reptiles are numerous in the ruins, among which a species of lizard called *Gubaira*, whose bite is deadly poisonous, must not be despised. The *Kala nag* (black cobra) is also frequently to be met with, and the writer during his short stay noticed two, one of which he killed at the Lāl Bungalow.[2] The reptile measured nearly five feet and was about one inch and a half thick.

The most convenient route to Mandū (22° 21′ N. Lat. and 75° 26′ E. Long.) is via Dhār, which is thirty-four miles by the direct road from Mhow and thirty from Indore.[3] Mandū is twenty-two miles south of Dhār.

[1] *Memoirs of Jahāngīr*, by Rogers and Beveridge, Oriental Translation Fund, New Series, vol. xix, pp. 383–4.

[2] For a description of this building see *infra*, pp. 106–8.

[3] Mhow and Indore are large Stations on the Khandwa and Ajmer Section of the B.B. & C.I. Ry. (Meter Gauge). Travellers

The roads are motorable, and omnibuses ply between Indore and Dhār, as well as between Mhow and Dhār. The visitor may also engage a special taxi-cab for Mandū at either Mhow or Indore Station.

from Bombay must change at Khandwa Junction (G.I.P. Ry.) for Indore or Mhow. There is an alternative route from Bombay by the B.B. & C.I. Ry. (Broad Gauge). Visitors travelling on this line must change at Ratlam for Indore.

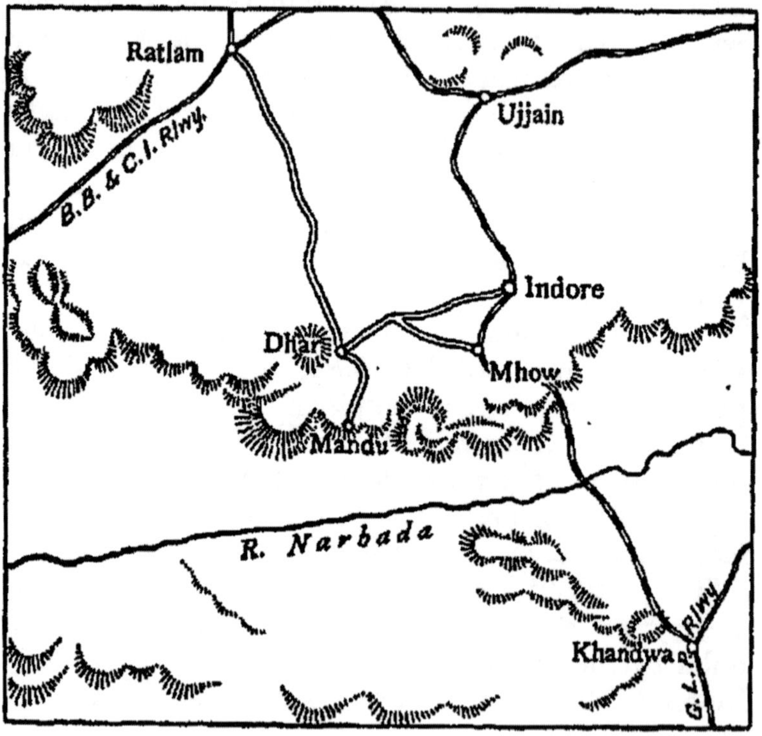

CHAPTER II

History

ABUL FAḌL narrates an amusing story in connexion with the building of Mandū. He writes: "Learned Hindus assert that a stone is met with in this country which when touched by any malleable metal turns it into gold, and they call it *Pāras*. They relate that before the time of Bikramajit, there reigned a just prince named Raja Jai Sing Deva who passed his life in deeds of beneficence. Such a stone was discovered in that age, and became the source of vast wealth. The sickle of a straw-cutter by its action was changed into gold. The man, not understanding the cause, thought that some damage had occurred to it. He took it to a blacksmith by name Māndan to have it remedied, who, divining its properties, took possession of it and amassed immense wealth. But his natural beneficence suggested to him that such a priceless treasure was more fitted for the reigning prince, and going to court he presented it. The Raja made it the occasion of many good deeds, and by means of the riches he acquired, completed this fort (Mandū) in twelve years, and at the request of the blacksmith the greater number of the stones with which it was built were shaped like an anvil. One day he held a festival on the banks of the Narbada, and promised to bestow a considerable fortune on his Brahman priest. As he had somewhat withdrawn his heart from worldly goods, he presented him with this stone. The Brahman from ignorance and meanness of soul became indignant and threw the precious treasure into the river, to his subsequent and eternal regret. Its depth there prevented his recovering it, and to this day that part of the river has never been fathomed.'[1]

The emperor Jahāngīr repeats the story in his *Memoirs*, but his critical mind could not accept it, so he remarks rather curtly: 'It appears to me to be all delusion.'[2] Firishta ascribes the building of Mandū to 'Anand-dew Rajpoot of the tribe of Beis, who lived in the age of Khoosrow Purvees (590–628) and died after a reign of sixteen years.'[3] The last-named historian's account of the early rajas of India is again based on legends and no great importance can be attached to his statement, but recently a copper-plate grant of Jayavarmadeva, dated A.D. 1261, has been found which mentions Mandū[4] as having been 'One of the last strongholds of the Paramāra Kings'.[5] The latter version is supported by the Hindu remains of Mandū, which, according to tradition or the style of architecture, can be placed between the tenth and thirteenth centuries A.D.,[6] the period of Paramāra supremacy in Malwa. The history of Mandū, which on account of its unique natural defences must have been a fortress from time immemorial, is unknown prior to the rule of the Paramāras (8th–13th centuries A.D.), and of that period also the data hitherto collected are too scanty to form a continuous account.

[1] *Jarrett's* English translation, vol. ii, p. 197.

[2] *Rogers and Beveridge*, vol. i, pp. 364–5.

[3] *Briggs*, vol. i, p. lxxx.

[4] It is mentioned as Mandapa-durga in the Sanskrit plates of the Paramāra period. *Annual Report*, A.S.I., 1903–4, p. 30.

[5] *Ibid.*

[6] The tank, Munja Talāo, is apparently after the name of the renowned Paramāra King Munja, who ruled in the latter part of the tenth century. Again the ruins of the Temple near the Lohānī Gate and the carved masonry of the ceiling of the Hindolā Mahall may range in period from the tenth to twelfth centuries A.D. (*infra*, pp. 72–122).

The Musalmans appeared on the scene in the second quarter of the thirteenth century, when Shams-ud-Dīn Iltutmish marched an army towards Malwa and conquered Ujjain, then the seat of government.[1] This invasion had apparently no lasting effect, for in 705 A.H. (A.D. 1305) 'Rai Mahlak Deo, of Malwa, and Koka, his Pradhan, forsake the path of obedience', thus giving umbrage to the Sulṭān, 'Ala-ud-Dīn Khaljī. A select army of royal troops was appointed, and the Sulṭān directed his confidential chamberlain, 'Ain-ul-Mulk, to expel Mahlak Deo from Mandū 'and to cleanse that old Gabristan from the stench of infidelity'. A spy showed 'Ain-ul-Mulk a way secretly into the fort (Mandū), and he advanced upon Mahlak Deo 'before even his household gods were aware of it'. The Rā'i was slain while attempting to fly, and Mandū was added to the government of 'Ain-ul-Mulk.[2]

Fitishta, on the other hand, places the first conquest of Malwa by the Musalmans during the reign of Ghīyāth-ud-Dīn Balban of Delhi (A.D. 1265–87), and observes that from that time the province acknowledged allegiance to the Sulṭāns of Delhi until the reign of Muḥammad Shāh (A.D. 1389–94), when the Governor, Dilāwar Khān Ghorī, acquired complete authority.[3]

The history of Mandū in the proper sense begins with the government of Dilāwar Khān, who assumed 'the white canopy and scarlet pavilion of royalty' in the year 804 A.H. (A.D. 1401),[4] after the disruption of the Delhi empire consequent upon the invasion of Tīmūr. The original name of Dilāwar Khān was Ḥusain, and his

[1] *Briggs*, vol. i, p. 193.

[2] *Tarīkh-i-'Alā'ī*, as translated by Elliot, vol. iii, pp. 76 and 550.

[3] *Briggs*, vol. iv, p. 68, and *Memoirs of Jahāngīr* (Rogers and Beveridge), vol. ii, p. 407.

[4] *Briggs*, vol. iv, p. 170.

forefathers came from Ghor and took service in the court of the Delhi Sulṭāns. Ḥusain came into notice during the reign of Fīroz Tughluq, and acquired the title of Dilāwar Khān (the Valiant Khān), which became so popular that it survived even after his adopting the regal title of 'Amīd Shāh Dā'ūd[1] on his declaring independence in Malwa. The government of the latter province was conferred on him by Sulṭān Muḥammad, the son of Fīroz Tughluq, in recognition of the services which Dilāwar Khān had rendered him when he was but a prince.[2]

Dilāwar Khān, although he considered Dhār to be the seat of his government, frequently visited Mandū, remaining there sometimes for months together.[3] He had an ambitious son Alp Khān, who on his accession assumed the title of Hoshang Shāh. Firishta states that Alp Khān did not approve the homage paid by Dilāwar Khān to Sulṭān Maḥmūd Tughluq of Delhi, when he was driven out of the capital by Amīr Tīmūr.[4] He retired to Mandū during the stay of Maḥmūd Tughluq in Malwa and laid the foundation of the celebrated fortress, which was afterwards completed during his reign.[5] The fortification and the improvement of Mandū seem to have well advanced during Dilāwar Khān's regime, for on the Tārāpūr Gate[6] an inscription is carved

[1] In the *Wakiat-i-Mushtaki* (Elliot, iv, 553) Dilāwar Khān is styled Amīn Shāh. This is apparently a mistake for 'Amīd Shāh, which title is mentioned by Jahāngīr (*Memoirs*, Rogers and Beveridge, vol. ii, p. 407) and also preserved in the inscriptions of the King carved on the Lāt Masjid at Dhār (*Epigraphia Indo-Moslemica*, 1909–10, pp. 11–12).

[2] *Firishta* (Persian text), vol. ii, pp. 461–2.

[3] *Briggs*, vol. iv, p. 168.

[4] Firishta writes that Dilāwar Khān assumed the royal titles at the instance of his son. *Ibid.*, p. 169. [5] *Idem.*

[6] In addition to the Tārāpūr Gate another building, which can

which mentions that it was built by Dilāwar Khān in 809 A.H. (A.D. 1406–7), when the city, apparently on account of its hilarious surroundings, had already been re-named as Shādīābād (or the City of Joy).[1] Another proof of the new City having become the favourite resort of Dilāwar Khān may be had from the text of the inscription carved on the Lāt Masjid at Dhār, which is dated Mandūgarh, showing that the King held his court at the latter place, when the design of the inscription was approved.[2]

In A.D. 1405 Dilāwar Khān died and Alp Khān ascended his father's throne under the title of *As-Sulṭān-ul-Ā'ẓam Ḥusām-ud-Dunya wad-Dīn Abu-l-Mujāhid Hoshang Shāh As-Sulṭān.*[3] He ruled Malwa for nearly twenty-seven years and extended his territory as far as Kālpī in the north and down to Kherla in the south, while to aggrandize his power towards the west he waged a continuous war with the kings of Gujarat. His ambition and warlike nature brought him into conflict with Sayyid Mubārak Shāh, King of Delhi (1421–33), Ibrāhīm Shāh Sharqī of Jaunpūr (1400–40), and

be attributed to Dilāwar Khān with certainty, is the mosque built at the back of the Jahāz Maḥall near the north end of the Royal enclosure. The building bears an inscription and is still associated with the name of Dilāwar Khān (*infra*, pp. 74–5). See also *Epigraphia Indo-Moslemica*, 1909–10, p. 20.

[1] *Ibid.*, p. 19. Firishta writes that it was Sulṭān Muḥammad Ghorī, the third King of Malwa, who gave Mandū the new title of Shādīābād, but the coins of his father, Hoshang Shāh, bear

Khān's reign. Vide *Briggs*, iv, 191, and Wright's *Catalogue of Coins in the Indian Museum*, Calcutta, vol. ii, pp. 246–7.

[2] *Epigraphia Indo-Moslemica*, 1909–10, p. 12.

[3] *Wright*, vol. ii, pp. 246–7.

[4] *Briggs*, vol. iv, pp. 172–85.

Aḥmad Shāh Baihmanī of Gulbarga (1422–35).[1] Mandū was besieged several times during Hoshang Shāh's reign, and at one time he was carried away prisoner by Muẓaffar Shāh of Gujarat, and one Nuṣrat Khān was appointed as Governor of Malwa. But fortune shortly afterwards smiled upon Hoshang, and he was released from confinement and reinstated on the throne of Malwa.[2]

A most daring piece of adventure was the expedition which he led against the Raja of Jājnagar (Orissa), in order to secure elephants for his army. Firishta has narrated it in considerable detail and I quote him here. 'In the year 825 (A.D. 1421) Hoshang left Mandū with one thousand chosen cavalry, assuming the character of a merchant, and marched to Jājnagar, one month's journey from Malwa. In order the better to conceal his object, he took with him horses of different colours, viz. bright bay, bright chestnut, and different shades of grey, such as the Prince of Jājnagar was known to admire most, and many other kinds of merchandise considered scarce in his country, which the King intended to barter for elephants. The pretended merchants having arrived, the Raja, according to the custom of his country, intimated his intention first of all to inspect the linen goods, and then either to purchase them with money or to barter elephants for them. The appointed day arrived, and the goods were spread out on the ground, but on account of the heavy appearance of the weather, Sulṭān Hoshang told the people that the articles would be damaged if rain came on. The Raja's servants, however, insisted on their remaining exposed till their master came, and at the same time the horses were all saddled for inspection. The Raja at length arrived, and a

[1] *Briggs*, vol. iv, pp. 183–5, and *Ā'īn-i-Akbarī* (Jarrett's translation), vol. ii, pp. 219–20.

[2] *Ibid.*, pp. 172–3.

thunder-storm coming on shortly after, the elephants of his cavalcade trampled over the merchandise, which was much damaged. Sulṭān Hoshang, smarting under the loss he had sustained, ordered his followers to mount, and without hesitation attacked the Raja's escort, many of whom were slain, and the Prince himself taken prisoner, after which Sulṭān Hoshang informed him of his real rank. Thus situated, the Raja of Jājnagar purchased his liberty with seventy-five large elephants, but Sulṭān Hoshang obliged him, as a measure of precaution, to accompany him as far as the confines of his country, whence he permitted him to return, but not without having received from him a few more of his finest elephants.'[1]

Hoshang with his warlike nature seems to have possessed a sympathetic heart for which his subjects adored him.[2] His tomb acquired sanctity shortly after his death and a large religious assembly ('Urs) used to be held at his mausoleum every year until quite recently, for the 'Bombay Subaltern' refers to it in his account published in 1844. Abul Faḍl, in the vein of a sceptic, disposes of the miracle—the rocks shedding tears on the King's death—attributed to the tomb of Hoshang Shāh during his time. He writes: 'A remarkable fact is that in summer time water trickles from the domed roof of the Mausoleum of Sulṭān Hoshang and the simple-minded have long regarded it as a prodigy, but the more acute of understanding can satisfactorily account for it.'[3] In

[1] *Briggs*, vol. iv, pp. 178–9, and *A'in* (Jarrett's translation), vol. ii, p. 219.

[2] He was also an impartial ruler. At Deogarh, near Lalitpūr in the United Provinces, an inscription of Saṃvat 1481 (A.D. 1424) records the dedication of two Jaina images during the reign of Shāh Alambhaka of Mandapapura, that is, of Shāh Alp Khān (Hoshang Shāh) of Mandū. Vide Campbell's *Mandū* (*J.B.R.A.S.* xix, 163).

[3] *A'in* (Jarrett's translation), vol. ii, p. 197. Firishta also on the

this age of disbelief the miracle has ceased to work, very much to the chagrin of pious votaries. Perhaps the discontinuance is due to the administration of lime to the open joints of the building, which had previously to this received a supply of divine moisture from the clouds to shed tears of mercy on the demise of the King!

The greatest claim for Hoshang's name to be transmitted to posterity is his fine taste for architecture, which made Mandū not only one of the most impregnable forts of India,[1] but also a magnificent city. He erected there a large number of stately edifices, among which the Great Mosque, the Delhi Darwāzah and his own tomb, for boldness of design and grace of finish,

basis of a history of Hoshang Shāh records this phenomenon, observing, 'Water constantly oozes from the sides of his vault, between the apertures of the masonry.' *Briggs*, iv, 190.

[1] Firishta and Emperor Jahāngīr have both referred to the defences of the Fort in eulogistic terms, and a quotation from the former may perhaps be of interest to readers. He writes: 'This fortification being one of the most extraordinary in the world, I think it proper in this place to give some description of it. It is built on the summit of an insulated mountain, said to be nineteen *coss* in circumference (28 miles). The place of a regular ditch is supplied by a deep ravine, formed by nature round the fortification, which is so deep that it seems impossible to take the fort by regular approaches. Within the fort is abundance of water and forage, though there is not sufficient space for the purposes of cultivation. Any army besieging Mandū must confine its operations chiefly to blockading the roads, for it is scarcely possible to invest a place of such extent. Many of the roads from the fort are steep, and difficult of access. That leading to the south, known by the name of the Tārāpūr Gate, is so rough and steep that cavalry can with difficulty find a way up, and on whatever side it is approached a pass must be surmounted, so that the enemy's force, though it occupies the several accessible roads, is necessarily divided, and one party may be cut off without receiving assistance from another. The road on the north leading to the Delhi Gate is by far the most easy of access.' *Briggs*, iv, 180–1.

take rank among the finest monuments in the East.[1] Sulṭān Hoshang had from the beginning evinced great partiality towards Malik Maḥmūd, the son of his cousin, Malik Mughīth, the minister,[2] and later the King conferred on him the title of Khān and appointed him the deputy of his father. He also directed that wherever he should take the field that young man should accompany him, while Malik Mughīth remained at the capital. Maḥmūd Khān thus gradually rose to power, and when the King fell dangerously ill and knew that his end was near, he proclaimed his eldest son, Prince Ghaznī Khān, his successor, 'and delivered him into the hands of Maḥmūd Khān, who promised to support the right of the Prince to the throne even to the last drop of his blood'.[3] On the 9th of Dhu Ḥajj, 835 H. (7 August, A.D. 1432), Sulṭān Hoshang expired,[4] and two days after that Ghaznī Khān ascended the throne at Mandū assuming the titles, *As-Sulṭān-ul-Ā'ẓam Tāj-ud-Dunya wad-Dīn Abu-l-Maḥāmid*,

[1] For a description of these buildings see *infra*, pp. 43–50.

[2] Malik Mughīth had espoused the cause of Sulṭān Hoshang against his rival Mūsa Khān, who was raised to the sovereignty of Malwa when Hoshang was carried away prisoner by Muẓaffar Shāh of Gujarat. Hoshang on his reinstatement appointed Malik Mughīth as his minister and retained implicit confidence in him throughout his reign. *Briggs*, iv, 174.

[3] *Ibid.*, pp. 177, 178, and 188.

[4] The last remains of Hoshang were first temporarily entombed at Hoshangābād. Briggs, who visited the place in October 1817, writes: 'The place of interment is still shown by some pious Mohammadans, who reside on the spot, and the lines commemorative of his death were legible.

شہہ والاقدر سلطان هوشنگ سوی دار البقا چون کرد آهنگ
بپرسیدم ز هاتف سال تاریخ ندا آمد نمانده شاه هوشنگ

Idem, p. 190.

Muḥammad Shāh as-Sulṭān.[1] Maḥmūd Khān showed much devotion to the King in the beginning, but later, when intrigue and jealousy put his own life in jeopardy, he felt no scruple in arranging for the murder of the King by bribing his cup-bearer, who administered poison in his wine.[2] This happened in 840 H. (A.D. 1436). Maḥmūd Khān, after this event, invited his father to assume the reins of government, but he declined, saying that he alone was best able to conduct the affairs of the State.[3]

Of the reign of Muḥammad Ghorī there is no monument at Mandū, except the Mosque of Malik Mughīth[4] to the east of the Sāgar lake, which has an inscription dated the 4th Rajab, 835 H. (7 March, A.D. 1432).[5] The anomaly about this record is that although it bears the above date, which is a few months earlier than the death of Hoshang Shāh (7 August, A.D. 1432), it mentions in the text the name of Maḥmūd Khaljī as that of the reigning King, though he did not assume the royal title until 1436.[6] The only explanation possible is that the mosque was begun during the last year of Hoshang's reign (835 H.—A.D. 1432), but was not completed until Maḥmūd Khaljī declared himself the King. The writer

[1] Wright's *Catalogue*, p. 247.

[2] For the intrigues and treacherous dealings of Muḥammad Ghorī's reign (A.D. 1432–6) the reader is referred to the *Wakiat-i-Mushtaki* (*Elliot*, iv, 552–4), as also to *Briggs*, iv, 192–4 and the *Ā'in* (Jarrett's translation), vol. ii, p. 220.

[3] Malik Mughīth always evinced great deference towards the descendants of his patron, Sulṭān Hoshang, and when during the reign of his son Maḥmūd disturbances arose in which the sons of the late king were involved, he interceded in their behalf and secured them pardon. *Ibid.*, pp. 194 and 197–8.

[4] For a description of this building see *infra*, pp. 82–6.

[5] *Epigraphia Indo-Moslemica*, 1909–10, p. 21.

[6] Wright's *Catalogue*, vol. ii, pp. 242 and 247.

of the inscription has therefore given the date of the commencement of the building correctly; but for the name of the reigning King, as he had to please the ruler who happened to be on the throne when the inscription was drafted, he has mentioned the name of Maḥmūd Khaljī.[1]

Maḥmūd Khaljī crowned himself with the royal tiara of Sulṭān Hoshang in 840 H. (A.D. 1436) and ordered public prayers to be read in his name and coins struck.[2] On this occasion he also presented robes of honour to the officers of the State, and on his father, who already enjoyed the distinguished denomination of *Malik-i-Ashraf Khān-i-Jahān*, he conferred the still higher titles of *Amīr-ul-Umarā* and *Ā'ẓam-i-Humāyūn*.[3] He further granted him the honour of using the white canopy and the silver quiver, exclusive marks of royalty, besides the privilege of being attended by gentlemen ushers, bearing golden and silver staves, who preceded him, when he appeared in public, proclaiming his titles, commencing 'By the grace of God' and so on.[4] Maḥmūd Khaljī bore very deep affection for his father and, when the latter died, during the siege of Mandisor, he became almost

[1] The coins of Muḥammad Ghorī bearing the royal title and the date 840 H. (A.D. 1436) are available at various museums, so there is no possibility of Maḥmūd Khaljī assuming the royal title in Rajab 835 H. (March, A.D. 1432) according to this inscription. For coins of Muḥammad Ghorī see Wright's *Catalogue*, vol. ii, p. 247.

[2] *Briggs*, iv, 196, and *Wright*, ii, 242. The titles of the King, as given on his coins, are *As-Sulṭān-ul-Ā'ẓam 'Ala-ud-Dunyā wad-Dīn Abu-l-Muẓaffar Maḥmūd Shāh Khaljī as-Sulṭān*, to which he subsequently added the more ambitious honorifics of *Sikandar-uth-Thānī* and *Yamīn-ul-Khilāfat Nāṣir-u-Amīr-il-Mominīn*.

[3] Briggs has not translated properly the Persian text regarding the titles of Malik Mughīth, I have therefore followed the original in this matter. Vide *Firishta* (Persian text), vol. ii, p. 479.

[4] *Briggs*, iv, 196.

distracted with grief and 'tore his hair and raved like one bereaved of his senses'.[1]

The first year or two of Maḥmūd Khaljī's reign were spent in disposing of rival claimants and resisting an invasion by Gujarat. Having made his position firm, he spent the greater part of his long reign of thirty-three years in extending his influence, and under him the kingdom of Malwa reached its widest limit. The neighbouring province of Mewar was the object of frequent expeditions which met with alternating success and defeat. Rana Kumbha was, however, forced to acknowledge the suzerainty of Malwa in 858 H. (A.D. 1454).[2] In memory of one of his victories over the Rana of Mewar, Maḥmūd Khaljī built at Mandū a lofty column, seven storeys high, of which only a fragment remains now.[3]

Maḥmūd Khaljī also reduced the minor states of Bundi, Kotah, Bīyana, Ranthambor, and Qarauli, to the north of his territory, and in 859 H. (A.D. 1454) conquered the principality of Mandisor and captured Ajmer as well.[4] War was waged against the independent rulers of Gujarat, Jaunpur, and the Deccan, and even the Delhi Sulṭān was not left alone.[5]

He was a great patron of learning and founded several

[1] *Briggs*, iv, p. 209. [2] *Ibid.*, 222.

[3] *Infra*, p. 58. [4] *Briggs*, iv, 222.

[5] Firishta narrates the cause of the Delhi expedition thus: 'In the year 844, Sulṭān Maḥmūd received petitions from the chiefs of Mewat and Delhi, stating that Syed Muḥammad, King of Delhi, the nephew and successor of Syed Mubārak, was totally incapable of supporting the weighty affairs of the government of his vast empire, that the oppressed were calling out on all sides for redress, and that the nation was anxious for Sulṭān Maḥmūd to march to Delhi, and ascend the throne. In consequence of these overtures, in the latter end of the same year, Sulṭān Maḥmūd put his army in motion for that purpose.' *Ibid.*, pp. 205–6, and *Elliot*, iv, 85.

colleges in different parts of his kingdom for the promotion of literature, as the result of which the philosophers and divines of Malwa bore a fair comparison with those of Shiraz and Samarqand.[1]

Firishta has commended the character of the King in no stinted terms, writing: 'Sulṭān Maḥmūd was polite, brave, just, and learned, and during his reign his subjects, Muhammadans as well as Hindus, were happy and maintained a friendly intercourse with each other. Scarcely a year passed that he did not take the field, so that his tent became his home, and his resting-place the field of battle. His leisure hours were devoted to hearing the histories and memoirs of the courts of different Kings of the earth read. He prided himself, not without reason, on his intimate knowledge of human nature, a subject to which he devoted much attention.'[2]

The fame of his military prowess and high personal qualities seems to have spread in the Islamic world, for embassies arrived at his court from Sulṭān Abū Sa'īd, the grandson of Tīmūr, who ruled in Transoxiana, and from the Amīr-ul-Mominīn Musta'id Bi'llah Yūsuf, the son of Muḥammad 'Abbāsī, the Caliph of Egypt. Flattered by these marks of attention he sent return embassies with a variety of rare presents such as 'muslins of all descriptions, Arab horses, dancing women and singers mounted on elephants superbly caparisoned, together with a number of Indian and Abyssinian slaves for the seraglio and also a few *Mainas*[3] and parrots which had been taught the Persian language'.[4]

[1] *Briggs*, iv, 197. [2] *Ibid.*, 234.

[3] The well-known Indian talking bird, with dark plumage intermixed with yellow and white spots.

[4] *Briggs*, vol. iv, pp. 229 and 232. Abu-l-Faḍl (Jarrett's translation of the *Ā'īn*, vol. ii, p. 220), writing about the embassy from

Maḥmūd Khaljī was also fond of architecture and, besides completing the Great Mosque and Tomb of Sulṭān Hoshang and repairing the palace of the same monarch, he erected a number of lofty structures at Mandū and elsewhere.[1] The most magnificent of these was his own tomb, built entirely of marble and standing on a higher plinth than those of the mausoleum and the Jāmi' Masjid of Hoshang. This lofty structure was already in a parlous condition during Akbar's reign, whose engineers repaired it in an inartistic manner by inserting patches of red stone in beautiful dados of white marble.[2]

Among the other works of Maḥmūd mention may be made of the College (now styled the Ashrafī Maḥall) which he founded opposite the Mosque of Sulṭān Hoshang and at one end of which (north-west angle) stood the beautiful victory column which he erected in commemoration of his victory over the Rana Kumbha of Mewar.[3] The building of the College seems to have been disturbed during Maḥmūd's time, for we notice that the basement for his tomb was provided by filling up the court forming the inner quadrangle of the College.[4] Maḥmūd's buildings were grand and lofty in design, but having been built in a hurry or under the superintendence of incompetent architects they fell down shortly after his reign and are now in ruins.

Firishta writes that in 849 H. (A.D. 1445) the Sulṭān

Sulṭān Abū Sa'īd, observes that it greatly redounded to the glory of Maḥmūd Khaljī.

[1] The King built some beautiful palaces and mosques at Nalcha (Na'lcha), a town on the way to Mandū from Dhār. In A.D. 1817 Sir John Malcolm (*Central India*, i, 32 *n.*) fitted up one of Maḥmūd's palaces as a hot-weather residence. Maḥmūd also built a palace of seven storeys at Fatḥabād. *Briggs*, iv, 213.

[2] *Infra*, pp. 59–61. [3] *Infra*, p. 58. [4] *Infra*, p. 57.

also founded a large hospital at Mandū and, having granted lands for its maintenance, appointed Faḍl Ullah, his own physician, to superintend the institution. This hospital was so well arranged that it included wards and attendants for all classes of patients and that the apartments for maniacs were separate from the rest.[1]

In 873 H. (A.D. 1469) Maḥmūd died on his way back from an expedition against Kachwāṛa, in the thirty-third year of his reign, and was succeeded by his eldest son, Ghiyāth-ud-Dīn.[2]

This king was very just and kind-hearted, and immediately on his accession to the throne he conferred on his younger brother, Fidwī Khān, the government of Ranthambor to be held in perpetuity, and appointed his own son, 'Abdu-l-Qādir, prime minister, proclaiming him also heir-apparent with the title of Sulṭān Nāṣir-ud-Dīn and the distinction of using the *chatr* and *palki* (royal canopy and palanquin).[3] Ghiyāth-ud-Dīn had rendered conspicuous service as a general during

[1] *Briggs*, iv, 214.

[2] *Ibid.*, p. 233. Firishta gives the following chronogram for the death of the King (19th Dhū Qā'dh, 873 H.):

شہی والاقدر سلطان محمود　　چون شه از امرحق رحلت لزینی

بپرسیدم ز ہاتف سال تاریخ　　ندا آمد که شد جنت نشینی

Translation

'When the illustrious Sulṭān Maḥmūd, according to the will of God, went on his long journey, I asked of a courtier the date of his death, and a voice answered, "He has a place in heaven".'

The numerals of the last two words جنت نشینی give the date of his death.

[3] *Briggs*, iv, 236. The legends on his coins show that Ghiyāth-ud-Dīn bore the following titles: Al-Wāthiq bi-l-Maliki-l-Multajī Abu-l-Fatḥ Ghiyāth Shāh Al-Khaljī. Vide *Wright*, ii, 250.

the various expeditions led by the late Sulṭān,[1] so, on taking up the reins of government, he declared that he would now yield up the sword to his son and pass his life in peaceful pursuits.[2] Historians have painted his character in contradictory lights accentuating the traits of his soft compassionate nature. He had undoubtedly a peculiar fancy for women, and established within his seraglio all the separate offices of a court, and had at one time fifteen thousand women in his service. Firishta writes: 'Among these were school mistresses, musicians, dancers, embroiderers, women to read prayers, and persons of all professions and trades. Five hundred beautiful young Turki females in men's clothes, and clad in uniform, armed with bows and quivers, stood on his right hand and were called the Turki guard. On his left were five hundred Abyssinian females also dressed in uniform and armed with fire-arms.'[3]

But notwithstanding this extraordinary fancy Ghiyāth-ud-Dīn was a deeply religious man and never missed his daily prayers,[4] nor did he ever taste wine or any intoxicating drug. In the *Wakiat-i-Mushtaki* an

[1] *Briggs*, pp. 206, 217–18, 221, and 224.

[2] *Idem.*, p. 236, and *Memoirs of Jahāngīr* (Rogers and Beveridge), vol. ii, p. 366.

[3] *Briggs*, iv, 236–7. Jahāngīr gives a similar account, adding a few more details. He writes: 'They say that he had collected 15,000 women in his harem. He had a whole city of them, and had made it up of all castes, kinds, and descriptions—artificers, magistrates, qazis, Kotwals, and whatever else is necessary for the administration of a town. Whenever he heard of a virgin possessed of beauty he would not desist until he possessed her. He taught the girls all kinds of arts and crafts, and was much given to hunt. He had made a deer park and collected all kinds of animals in it. He often used to hunt in it with his women.' Vide *Rogers and Beveridge*, vol. ii, pp. 366–7.

[4] *Ibid.*, 237, and *Elliot*, iv, 555.

amusing story is given to show his abhorrence of intoxicants, which may be quoted here. 'One day a potion (*mā'jūn*) was made for him, and when it was ready he was informed of it. He said it was not to be brought to him until he had heard the names of the ingredients in it. Accordingly, the list was brought and read to him. He heard it. There were three hundred and more ingredients in it, and among them was one drachm of nutmeg. He said the medicine was of no use to him. More than a lac of *tankas* had been spent for it, but he ordered it to be brought and thrown into the drain. A person begged that it might be given to somebody else, but he replied, what he could not allow himself to take, he would not give to others.'[1]

Ghiyāth-ud-Dīn enjoyed the result of the various treaties[2] which were concluded with the neighbouring powers during his father's time, and no invasion of the Malwa kingdom occurred during his reign, except the attack of Ranthambor by Bahlol Lodī, King of Delhi. This was effectively repulsed and Bahlol so chastised that he thought it advisable to pay a sum of money as ransom.[3]

The author of the *Mirat-i-Sikandari*, referring to Ghiyāth-ud-Dīn, has written that he ruled in Mandū with order and liberality,[4] which opinion is confirmed by the various tales of his justice and charity, extending even to animals and birds, given by different historians.[5]

[1] *Elliot*, iv, 555. [2] *Briggs*, vol. iv, pp. 213–14, 222 and 230.
[3] *Ibid.*, iv, 237–8. [4] Bayley's *Gujarat*, p. 169.
[5] Firishta writes: 'One day having observed a mouse in the royal apartment, he ordered it to receive its daily allowance of rice and money; and this absurdity extended to the tame pigeons, parrots, &c.' Vide *Briggs*, iv, 237. The reader is also referred to the *Wakiat-i-Mushtaki* (*Elliot*, iv, 555), wherein some pleasant stories of the King's piety and bounty are given.

Near the end of his reign rivalry sprang up between his youngest son Shuja't Khān and Nāṣir-ud-Dīn, the heir apparent, and it rose to such a pitch that Nāṣir, fearing that his brother might be depriving him of his claim to the throne, administered poison to the aged King. Jahāngīr has narrated the event most feelingly: 'It is well known that that wretch (Nāṣir-ud-Dīn) advanced himself by the murder of his own father, Ghiyāth-ud-Dīn, who was in his eightieth year. Twice he gave him poison, and he twice expelled it by means of a *zabr-muhra* (poison antidote, bezoar) he had on his arm. The third time he mixed poison in a cup of *sherbet* and gave it to his father with his own hand, saying he must drink it. As his father understood what efforts he was making in this matter, he loosened the *zabr-muhra* from his arm and threw it before him, and then turning his face in humility and supplication towards the throne of the Creator, who requires no supplication, said: "O Lord, my age has arrived at eighty years, and I have passed this time in prosperity and happiness such as has been attained to by no king. Now as this is my last time, I hope that Thou wilt not seize Nāṣir for my murder, and that reckoning my death as a thing decreed Thou wilt not avenge it." After he had spoken these words, he drank off that poisoned cup of *sherbet* at a gulp and delivered his soul to the Creator.'[1]

Firishta has tried to absolve Nāṣir-ud-Dīn from the charge of parricide by asserting that no circumstance was brought forward to prove the crime, nor does there appear any motive that should have actuated him to commit such an act, as he had already been declared heir apparent by his father's consent and had long conducted, without restraint, the affairs of the government.[2]

[1] *Rogers and Beveridge*, ii, 365–6.

[2] *Briggs*, iv, 240.

The treatment offered to the last remains of Nāṣir by Sher Shāh as well as by Jahāngīr, both of whom visited Mandū and had reliable information at their disposal, however, leaves no doubt that Nāṣir was guilty of the crime.[1]

Ghiyāth-ud-Dīn having resided throughout his long reign at Mandū must have adorned the capital with a number of buildings. The picturesque palace, Jahāz Maḥall, with its beautiful adjuncts, in view of the refined taste of the King and his love of enjoyment, may be safely attributed to him.[2]

Nāṣir-ud-Dīn proclaimed himself as the King of Malwa on the 27th Rabī' II, 906 H. (20 November, A.D. 1500).[3] His accession was attended by a series of domestic feuds in which many of the nobles were involved. Of these Sher Khān, Governor of Chanderi, Sikandar Khān of Erich, and Mahābat Khān of Mandisor, making common cause, marched against the King, but the rebels were defeated and Sher Khān and Sikandar Khān killed in the action.[4]

[1] Jahāngīr writes: 'It is reported that when Sher Khān, the Afghan, in the time of his rule, came to the tomb of Nāṣir-ud-Dīn, he, in spite of his brutish nature, on account of Nāṣir-ud-Dīn's shameful conduct, ordered the head of the tomb to be beaten with sticks. Also when I went to his tomb I gave it several kicks, and ordered the servants in attendance on me to kick the tomb. Not satisfied with this, I ordered the tomb to be broken open and his impure remains to be thrown into the fire. Then it occurred to me that since fire is Light, it was a pity for the Light of Allāh to be polluted with burning his filthy body, also, lest there should be any diminution of torture for him in another state from being thus burnt, I ordered them to throw his crumbled bones, together with his decayed limbs, into the Narbada.' Vide *Rogers and Beveridge*, ii, 367.

[2] *Infra*, pp. 63–8.

[3] *Briggs*, iv, 241. The legend on the coins of this King reads thus: *Al-Wāthiq bi-ṣ-Ṣamad-i-lamyazalī Abu-l-Muẓaffar Nāṣir Shāh bin Ghiyāth Shāh al-Khaljī*. Vide *Wright*, ii, 253.

[4] *Ibid.*, iv, 241–2.

In the year 908 H. (A.D. 1502) troubles seem to have arisen also in Kachwara, where the King marched in person and punished the refractory Rajputs.[1] In the following year, viz. 909 H. (A.D. 1503), he led an expedition towards Chitor, where, having received a large present in money from the Rana, he married a Rajput princess,[2] to whom he gave the title of Queen of Chitor.[3]

As since the time of Maḥmūd Khaljī the rulers of Khandesh had owned allegiance to the kings of Malwa, Nāṣir-ud-Dīn deputed a large force to repulse the army of Aḥmad Niẓām Shāh Baiḥrī, who had declared war against Dā'ūd Khān of Khandesh. But before the troops of Malwa reached their destination Aḥmad Niẓām Shāh retreated to Ahmadnagar and public prayers were read in the name of Nāṣir-ud-Dīn at Burhanpur.[4]

Although the King maintained order in his dominions he was a dipsomaniac and often committed acts of violence when in his cups. It is said that one day while lying in a state of intoxication on the verge of a reservoir of water, he fell in. Four female slaves, who were standing by, at the risk of their own lives pulled him out, and taking off his wet clothes dressed him again. On recovering from his intoxication he complained of violent headache, and the female slaves mentioned the circumstance of his falling into the reservoir in order to account for it. The King, however, was so enraged, conceiving it to be untrue, and that the females only said so by way of reproaching him for his inebriety, that he drew his sword and put them all to death with his own hand, in spite of their cries for mercy, and

[1] *Briggs*, iv, 243. [2] She was the daughter of Raja Jīwan Dās.
[3] *Ibid.* [4] *Idem.*

although they exhibited the wet clothes which they had taken off him.[1]

During the latter part of his reign, the demon of filial ingratitude seems to have preyed heavily upon his mind and therefore he became suspicious of his own sons. This feeling grew so apparent that Prince Shihāb-ud-Dīn, the heir apparent, dreading the wrath of his father, fled to Delhi and refused to come back in spite of the remonstrances of the latter.[2]

In 916 H. (A.D. 1510) Nāṣir-ud-Dīn died of a burning fever, which he had apparently contracted by his evil habits.[3] Firishta writes that the King had shown keen penitence before his death and bequeathed his kingdom to his third son, Maḥmūd.[4]

Nāṣir-ud-Dīn was fond of building and he erected a magnificent palace at Akbarpur,[5] which according to Firishta was much admired by all who saw it.[6] He also built the beautiful palace near Rīwā Kund, now accredited to Bāz Bahādur.[7]

[1] *Briggs*, iv, 242–3; *Elliot*, vi, 350; and *Rogers and Beveridge*, ii, 367.

[2] *Ibid.*, 244.

[3] *Ibid.* In the *Wakiat-i-Jahangiri* it is, however, stated that Nāṣir-ud-Dīn was drowned. Vide *Elliot*, vi, 350.

[4] *Firishta* (Persian text), vol. ii, pp. 517–18.

[5] Campbell (*J.B.R.A.S.* xix, 173) has identified Akbarpur with the village of that name on the south bank of the Narbada about fifteen miles from Mandū. But Barnes (*ibid.*, xxi, 28 *n.*) in this connexion observes: 'It is difficult to locate this place. It is true there are ruins of what was evidently once a fort, but these ruins have no suggestion of magnificence, and bear no resemblance to those of Mandū. Moreover, the Kachwara country lies far to the north of Mandū; the Chiefs of Raghugarh being the present descendants of the old Kachwara Rajputs who troubled so much the Kings of Malwa.' Barnes's objection seems to be sound and the locality of Akbarpur should be traced somewhere in the Kachwara country.

[6] *Briggs*, iv, 243.

[7] *Epigraphia Indo-Moslemica*, 1909–10, p. 24; see also *infra*, pp. 92–7.

In 916 H. (A.D. 1510) Sulṭān Maḥmūd II crowned himself with great pomp and glory, 'on which occasion no fewer than seven hundred elephants, with velvet housings embroidered in gold, formed part of the procession'.[1] But shortly after his accession conspiracies were planned against him and rival princes acclaimed as Kings. Sulṭān Sikandar Lodī of Delhi[2] and Muẓaffar Shāh II of Gujarat espoused the cause of the elder brother of Maḥmūd, Ṣāḥib Khān, who assumed the title of Muḥammad II,[3] while the chief of Khandesh tried to help the claim of Shihāb-ud-Dīn and, when the latter died, the title of his son to the throne was proclaimed under the name of Hoshang II.[4] In these feuds a Rajput Chief, Mednī Rā'i, rendered most valuable service to Maḥmūd II and thus gained undue influence over the King.[5] The power of Mednī Rā'i ultimately became a real menace to him and he was obliged to take refuge with Muẓaffar Shāh II of Gujarat.[6] The latter King treated Maḥmūd II generously and led an expedition in person to oust Mednī Rā'i and to reinstate Maḥmūd II on the throne of Malwa. This was successfully accomplished,[7] but Maḥmūd in the reign of Muẓaffar II's suc-

[1] *Briggs*, iv, 246.

[2] Sikandar Lodī really endeavoured to get Malwa for himself, for an attempt to assert his supremacy was actually made by some of the officers of Sikandar Lodī which caused a breach between the Delhi Sulṭān and Ṣāḥib Khān's party, and this ended in the retreat of the former to Delhi. *Bayley*, p. 252 *n.*, and *Briggs*, iv, 252–6.

[3] The copper coins of Muḥammad II are preserved in the cabinets of various museums. Vide *Wright*, ii, 259.

[4] *Briggs*, iv, 250.

[5] *Ibid.*, pp. 247–62, and *Bayley*, pp. 255–61.

[6] *Ibid.*

[7] *Briggs*, iv, 257–62; *Bayley* (Gujarat), pp. 254–61; and *Elliot*, iv, 386. The *Mirat-i-Sikandari* gives a vivid description of the banquet which Maḥmūd gave to Muẓaffar Shāh on this occasion.

cessor, Bahādur Shāh, intrigued with the rival prince, Chānd Khān, and incurred displeasure. Bahādur Shāh marched towards Mandū and laid siege to the Fort, ultimately conquering it on the 9th Shā'bān, 932 H. (21 May, A.D. 1526).[1] Maḥmūd was taken prisoner and sent to the fort of Champaner for confinement, but on the way the troops carrying Maḥmūd were attacked by a party of Bhils, and the Gujarat general, Āṣaf Khān, suspecting that the attack was made to effect the release of Maḥmūd, ordered the King and his son to be put to death.[2] This happened on the 14th of Shā'bān, 932 H. (26 May, A.D. 1526), and the kingdom of Malwa was subsequently incorporated with that of Gujarat.

Maḥmūd II was brave and courageous, but also highly credulous and most indiscreet in matters of administration, and the latter shortcomings ultimately led to his ruin.[3]

It mentions: 'On the eleventh of Ṣafar, Sulṭān Muẓaffar visited the fort, and all the people of the city, in enormous bands, great and small, male and female, came out to see him, standing on the walls and on the house-tops, and expressed their thanks and blessings. Sulṭān Maḥmūd entertained him most sumptuously. After the banquet he conducted him round the palace. Unexpectedly they entered a building in which there was a quadrangle, painted and gilded, with rooms all round. As soon as they were in the middle the doors of all the rooms opened, and the women of Sulṭān Maḥmūd appeared at them, beautifully dressed and adorned, and looking like *ḥūrīs* and *parīs*. They brought plates full of gems and golden ornaments like the peacocks of Heaven, for Sulṭān Muẓaffar. Sulṭān Muẓaffar, when he saw them, said, "To look on what is unlawful is a crime". Sulṭān Maḥmūd said that they and all he had were at Sulṭān Muẓaffar's disposal. The latter thanked him, but begged that they might return within the *pardah*; and at a signal they all instantly disappeared like fairies.' Vide *Bayley*, pp. 260–1.

[1] *Briggs*, iv, 265–9, and *Bayley*, pp. 349–53.

[2] *Briggs*, iv, 269. Maḥmūd II was buried in the vicinity of the tank at Dohad.

[3] *Ibid.*, pp. 246–68.

Among the monuments of Mandū, the two buildings styled Gadā Shāh's House and Gadā Shāh's Shop[1] were perhaps built during Maḥmūd II's reign by Mednī Rā'i, the *de facto* ruler of Malwa. The former of these two buildings is situated in the royal enclosure and contains two paintings, representing a chief and a queen, which may be identified with Mednī Rā'i and his consort.[2]

The building styled Daryā Khān's tomb was also probably built during Maḥmūd's reign, for an officer called Daryā Khān Lodī was employed at his court.[3] Malwa remained a dependency of Gujarat till 941 H. (A.D. 1534) when Humāyūn conquered the Fort of Mandū, having scaled its walls by means of ladders and ropes somewhere near the Tārāpūr Gate. Sulṭān Bahādur, who had shut himself up in the Fort, was asleep when the Imperial army, jumping down from the walls, opened the gates and brought in their horses. The cries of Mallū Khān, an officer of the late Khaljī government, aroused Bahādur, who rushed out with a few attendants to attack Humāyūn's troops. Afterwards he made his way towards Songarh, the Citadel of Mandū, and having let his horses down the precipice by ropes, escaped to Champaner.[4] Humāyūn subsequently took up his residence at Mandū, when he cleared the province of rebels, settled the affairs of the conquered country of Gujarat, and suppressed the revolts in the vicinity of the capital.[5] But when he returned to Agra, Mallū Khān retook all the country between the Narbada and the town of Bhilsa, after a struggle of twelve months against the

[1] Shāh is apparently a corrupt form of the Hindu term *Sāh*, from which we get the title *Sāhū* generally given to bankers. In Persian writings this term is often written as *Sheh*, from which the modern title *Seth* is derived.

[2] *Infra*, pp. 80–1.

[3] *Briggs*, iv, 267, and *Bayley*, p. 349.

[4] *Elliot*, vi, 14, and *Briggs*, iv, 271.

[5] *Elliot*, vi, 15.

Delhi officers, and caused himself to be crowned in Mandū under the title of Qādir Shāh in 943 H. (A.D. 1536).[1] He ruled Malwa for nearly six years, till 949 H. (A.D. 1542), when Sher Shāh, who had established himself upon the throne of Delhi, marched upon Mandū. Qādir Shāh, finding his resources incapable of resisting the invading forces, threw himself on the mercy of Sher Shāh, but the latter appointed his minister and relative, Shujā' Khān, as governor of Malwa, giving over to him the country round Ujjain and Sarangpur.[2]

Shujā' Khān was an accomplished soldier and he successfully quelled the rebellion which arose in Malwa owing to the machinations of Qādir Shāh. Shujā' Khān ruled Malwa till 962 H. (A.D. 1554), when he died, although for a short time, owing to some misunderstanding between him and Salīm Shāh, the son of Sher

[1] *Briggs*, iv, 271. According to the *Mirat-i-Sikandari* (Persian text, p. 298) Mallū received his title of Qādir Shāh from Sulṭān Maḥmūd III of Gujarat (A.D. 1536–44), on the recommendation of his minister, 'Imād-ul-Mulk, who was a great friend of Mallū.

[2] *Briggs*, iv, 271–2. Firishta thus accounts for the invasion of Malwa by Sher Shāh: 'Shortly after his accession, Qādir Shāh received a *firman*, with a seal on the face of it, from Sher Shāh Purbī Afghan, King of Bengal, stating that Humāyūn Pādshāh was on the march to attack him, and that he desired the King of Malwa to make a movement towards Agra, which would distract the operations of the King of Delhi, and give the former an opportunity of acting with effect on that monarch's territory. On the receipt of this *firman* or order, Qādir Shāh was so incensed that he insisted on his secretary writing a *firman* in return with the seal upon the face of it (indicating his superiority over Sher Shāh). When Sher Shāh received the answer, he tore off the seal, and putting it on the point of his sword, said, "If it please God that I should ever meet Qādir Shāh, I will then put him in mind of his impertinence in putting his seal on the face of a letter to my address", and in consequence, when he ascended the throne of Delhi he marched to conquer Malwa.' *Ibid.*

Shāh, he was deprived of his governorship and 'Isā Khān appointed in his place. He was shortly afterwards reinstated, and Firishta writes that, when Humāyūn re-established himself on the throne of Delhi, Shujā' Khān was on the point of declaring himself independent and of coining money, but 'a cruel fate snatched the cup of prosperity from his lips and death presented him with the potion of mortality'.[1]

Shujā' Khān,[2] during his lifetime, had divided his territory among his sons, Daulat Khān, Malik Bāyazīd, and Muṣṭafa Khān. On the death of Shujā' Khān, Malik Bāyazīd treacherously killed his brother Daulat Khān and crowned himself as the independent ruler of Malwa, assuming the title of Sulṭān Bāz Bahādur in 963 H. (A.D. 1555).[3]

Bāz Bahādur was a gallant king and he took possession of many towns in Malwa which were previously almost independent; but later he sustained such a disgraceful defeat from Ranī Durgawatī that he forswore fighting. Firishta writes that at this period the science of music had attained considerable perfection in Malwa, and Bāz Bahādur devoted himself entirely to its cultivation and encouragement, and his attachment to Rūpmatī, a celebrated courtesan of that age, became so notorious, that the loves of Bāz Bahādur and Rūpmatī have been handed down to posterity in song.[4] Akbar,

[1] *Idem*, p. 275.

[2] Shuja' Khān has been styled Shujā'at Khān and also Shujāwal Khān by some historians. Firishta writes that among the public works which do credit to Shujā' Khān's memory is the town of Shujāwalpūr near Ujjain (*Briggs*, iv, 276) and the *Tarikh-i-Alfi* (*Elliot*, v, 168).

[3] *Briggs*, iv, 276.

[4] *Ibid.*, 277–8. Mr. L. M. Crump recently discovered a Persian manuscript containing the life-history of Rūpmatī, which he has translated into English together with the songs attributed to

taking advantage of this state of Malwa under Bāz Bahādur, ordered an army commanded by Adham Khān, in the latter end of the year 968 H. (A.D. 1561), to march and occupy that country. Niẓām-ud-Dīn, the author of the *Tabakat-i-Akbari*, has described this expedition in detail and he may be quoted here: 'Bāz Bahādur was the most accomplished man of his day in the science of music and in Hindī song. He spent much of his time in the society of singers and musicians. When the Imperial army was but ten *kos* from Sarangpur, Adham Khān sent forward an advanced force to the entrenchments which Bāz Bahādur had thrown up around his army. Several attempts were made to entice him out of his lines, and the royal forces drew together in order to surround him. Bāz Bahādur then threw off his apathy, and marched out to give battle. But the Afghan nobles in his army were disaffected, and withdrew, and he himself was obliged to fly. Rūpmatī, his favourite wife, who used to recite poetry, several other wives, and all his treasure fell into the hands of the Imperial forces. As the fugitives were escaping, a eunuch of Bāz Bahādur wounded Rūpmatī with a sword, to prevent her falling into the hands of strangers; and, when Adham Khān summoned her to his presence, she committed suicide by poisoning herself.'[1]

Adham Khān, shortly after this victory, was called back to Delhi and Pīr Muḥammad Khān appointed in his place as the Governor of Malwa. In A.D. 1561 Bāz Bahādur, with the help of Mīrān Mubārak Khān of Khandesh, gave a crushing defeat to Pīr Muḥammad

Rūpmatī. Vide *Lady of the Lotus*, Oxford University Press, 1926.

[1] *Elliot*, v, 270–1. *Firishta* (Persian text, ii, 540–1) has described this event with great poetic zest and skill.

Khan, who was slain in the action, and the Mughal troops were driven out of Malwa.[1] Akbar, on receiving the news of this disaster, deputed 'Abdullāh Khān to punish Bāz Bahādur, and the former marched upon Malwa towards the end of the year 969 H. (A.D. 1562). Bāz Bahādur, being unable to withstand the Mughal force, fled to the hills of Gondwara. Afterwards he found protection for some time with Rana Udi Singh of Mewar, whence he repaired to Gujarat, but eventually he threw himself upon the mercy of Akbar. The Emperor granted him a *mansab* of 2,000.[2]

Among the monuments of Mandū, ascribed to Bāz Bahādur, mention may be made of the beautiful reservoir, Rīwā Kund,[3] and of the palace close by and also

[1] *Briggs*, iv, 278–9.

[2] *Elliot*, v, 275–6, and the *Ā'īn* (Blochmann), i, 428.

[3] About the Rīwā Kund the following story is related: 'Bāz Bahādur was one day hunting in the forest bordering the right bank of the Narbada. Having outridden all his retinue he was in eager pursuit, when his ear was attracted by the most exquisite flood of melody from a neighbouring glade. He followed the sound and soon reached the spot, where seated 'neath a *bargat* tree a young Hindu maiden was singing to the woods and to the deer and birds which had thronged thither to listen to her voice. He was dazzled by her beauty and enchanted by her unrivalled song. Her conversation riveted his love. He strove to win her heart and hand. The first was speedily his, but the splendid lot to which he wooed her could not tempt her to dishonour the sacred race from which she sprang. She replied to all his overtures: "When the Narbada shall flow through Mandū, I will be thy bride, but not till then." Bāz Bahādur determined that the river should obey the voice of love, and climb the mountain height. He assembled the strength of his kingdom, axe in hand, to try the force of art. The river god, dreading to measure his strength against the majesty of love, rose before the astonished people in the form of a giant, whose forehead was lost in the skies. "Desist", he cried, "from thy rash attempt, but receive the well-merited reward of thy love, repair to Mandū, to a spot which overlooks

of the pavilions built on the crest of the southern ridge which are associated with the name of his consort Rūpmatī. According to the inscriptions carved on the two last-named buildings, they seem to have been built by earlier kings, and Bāz Bahādur apparently extended them.[1]

Akbar visited Mandū no less than four times during his reign. First, in A.D. 1573, when Adham Khān had shown signs of revolt and he marched in person to chastise him. The Imperial army reached Mandū on the new moon of Dhu-l-Ḥajj, 991 H. Akbar during this visit seems to have enjoyed the hilarity of spirit peculiar to the traditions of the place, for he sent a *firman* to Mubārak Shāh of Khandesh directing him 'to send any one of his daughters whom he thought worthy to attend upon the Emperor'. Mubārak Shāh received this message with great delight and sent his daughter with a suitable retinue and paraphernalia to the Emperor.[2]

Akbar visited Mandū for the second time in A.D. 1592, when his son Murād was appointed Governor of Malwa, and he halted there on his way to the Deccan.

His third and fourth visits also were in connexion with his expeditions to the Deccan, and of these there is an authentic record at Mandū in the shape of two inscriptions (dated 1008 and 1009 H.—A.D. 1600–1),[3]

our flood, search there for our sacred tamarisk and dig wherever it is found, beneath it, thou shalt come to a pure spring which, being tributary to us, is part of our divinity. Thither bear thy bride, to live as she has often sworn to live, upon the borders of her natal river." The King obeyed, he found the tamarisk and the spring, he dug the reservoir, he built near it a palace, and constructed a fine aqueduct to lead the waters of the fountain to the baths of the palace.' Vide *J.B.R.A.S.*, xxi, p. 371.

[1] *Infra*, pp. 92–100. [2] *Elliot*, v, 289–90.

[3] *Epigraphia Indo-Moslemica*, 1909–10, pp. 26–7.

carved on the walls of the delightful palace styled Nīl Kanth, built by Shāh Budāgh Khān, a governor of Mandū.[1]

Of Akbar's reign there are two more inscriptions in Mandū, one recording the repairs of the royal approach near the Tārāpūr Gate,[2] and the other the restoration of the tomb of Maḥmūd Khaljī already referred to (*supra*, p. 18).

With the extinction of the Khaljī dynasty of Malwa the glory of Mandū seems to have departed, but it enjoyed a respite, first during the six years' rule of Bāz Bahādur, and later during the reign of Jahāngīr, when the Emperor visited the Fort and had its old edifices repaired and also new ones built.[3] Jahāngīr stayed at Mandū for a little over seven months, arriving there on the 6th March 1617, and leaving on the 24th October of the same year.[4] During this period Mandū was the scene of several brilliant functions the account of which is preserved in the Emperor's own *Memoirs*, as also in the several histories of the embassy of Sir Thomas Roe, who visited Mandū with the Emperor.

Of the feast of the Shab-i-Barāt the Emperor writes: 'On Thursday evening, the 26th, corresponding with

[1] Budāgh Khān was appointed Governor of Mandū in A.D. 1568. Emperor Jahāngīr (*Memoirs*, Persian text, p. 372) thus describes his visit to the Nīl Kanth: 'On the third day of Amurdad (July, 1617), with the palace ladies I set out to see Nīl Kanth, which is one of the pleasantest places in Mandū fort. Shāh Budāgh Khān, who was one of the trusted nobles of my august father, built this very pleasing and joy-giving lodge, during the time he held this province in fief (A.D. 1572–7). I remained at Nīl Kanth till about an hour after nightfall and then returned to my State quarters.'

[2] *Epigraphia Indo-Moslemica*, 1909–10, p. 19.

[3] *Rogers and Beveridge*, ii, 363–4. Jahāngīr spent 3 lacs of rupees on repairs and new buildings.

[4] Kerr's *Voyages*, ix, 335, and *Elliot*, vi, 377.

the 14th Shā'bān, which is the Shab-i-Barāt, I held a meeting in one of the houses of the palace of Nūr Jahān Begam, which was situated in the midst of large tanks, and summoning the Amirs and courtiers to the feast which had been prepared by the Begam, I ordered the attendants to supply the guests with whatever intoxicating drinks they called for. Many asked for drinks, and I ordered that whoever did so should sit according to his *manṣab* and condition. All sorts of roast meats, and fruits by way of relish, were ordered to be placed before every one. It was a wonderful assembly. In the beginning of the evening they lighted lanterns and lamps all round the tanks and buildings, and a lighting-up was carried out the like of which has perhaps never been arranged in any place. The lanterns and lamps cast their reflection on the water, and it appeared as if the whole surface of the tank was a plain of fire. A grand entertainment took place, and the drunkards indulged themselves to excess.

A feast was arranged that lighted up the heart,
It was of such beauty as the heart desired.
They flung over this verdant mead
A carpet broad as the field of genius.
From abundance of perfume the feast spread far,
The heavens were a musk-bag by reason of incense,
The delicate ones of the garden (the flowers) became
glorious,
The face of each was lighted up like a lamp.'[1]

Mandū abounding in big game, the sporting instincts of the Emperor were fully gratified and numerous entries regarding his shooting expeditions occur in the *Memoirs*, one of which may be quoted here: 'On the 7th, as the huntsmen had marked down four tigers, when

[1] *Rogers and Beveridge*, ii, 385.

two watches and three *gharīs* had passed I went out to hunt them with my ladies. When the tigers came in sight Nūr Jahān Begam submitted that if I would order her she herself would kill the tigers with her gun. I said, "Let it be so." She shot two tigers with one shot each and knocked over the two others with four shots. In the twinkling of an eye she deprived of life the bodies of these four tigers. Until now such shooting was never seen, that from the top of an elephant and inside of a *howdah* six shots should be made and not one miss, so that the four beasts found no opportunity to spring or move. As a reward for this good shooting I gave her a pair of bracelets of diamonds worth 100,000 rupees and scattered 1,000 *ashrafīs* (over her).'[1]

The 1st September 1617 was Jahāngīr's birthday. Campbell has given the following account, based on Roe, Terry, and Corryat's statements: 'The king was forty-five years old, of middle height, stout but proportionately built, and of olive complexion. Roe went to pay his respects and was conducted apparently to Bāz Bahādur's gardens to the east of the Rīwā Pool. This tangled orchard was then a beautiful garden with a great square pond or tank set all round with trees and flowers, and in the middle of the garden a pavilion or pleasure-house under which hung the scales in which the king was to be weighed. The scales were of beaten gold set with many small stones, as rubies and turquoises. They were hung by chains of gold, large and massive, but strengthened by silken ropes. The beam and tressels from which the scales hung were covered with thin plates of gold. All round were the nobles of the court seated on rich carpets waiting for the king. He came laden with diamonds, rubies, pearls, and other precious

[1] *Rogers and Beveridge*, ii, 375.

vanities, making a great and glorious show. His swords, targets, and throne were equally rich and splendid. His head, neck, breast, and arms above the elbows and at the wrist were decked with chains of precious stones, and every finger had two or three rich rings. His legs were as it were fettered with chains of diamonds and rubies as large as walnuts and amazingly large pearls. He got into the scales crouching or sitting on his legs like a woman. To counterpoise his weight bags said to contain Rs. 9,000 in silver were changed six times. After this he was weighed against bags containing gold, jewels, and precious stones. Then against cloth of gold, silk stuffs, cotton goods, spices, and all commodities. Last of all against meal, butter, and corn. Except the silver, which was reserved for the poor, all was said to be distributed to Baniahs (that is, Brahmans). After he was weighed Jahāngīr ascended the throne and had basins of nuts, almonds, and spices of all sorts given him. These the king threw about, and his great men scrambled for them on all fours. Roe thought it not decent that he should scramble. And the king seeing that he stood aloof reached him a basin almost full and poured the contents into his cloak. The physicians noted the king's weight and spoke flatteringly of it. Then the Mughal drank to his nobles in his royal wine and the nobles pledged his health. The king drank also to the Lord Ambassador, whom he always treated with special consideration, and presented him with the cup of gold curiously enamelled and crusted with rubies, turquoises, and emeralds.'[1]

[1] *J.B.R.A.S.*, xix, 194–5. The works quoted by Campbell in this connexion are: (1) Roe in Kerr's *Voyages*, ix, 337–43; (2) Pinkerton's *Voyages*, viii, 35; (3) Terry's *Voyages*, pp. 377 and 403; and (4) Corryat's *Crudities*, iii, L. 2 (extracts unpaged).

Shāhjahān visited Mandū twice, first on the 2nd October 1617,[1] during his father's stay there, on which occasion he presented some magnificent jewels to his father the Emperor,[2] and again in 1621, when he was sum-

[1] Pinkerton's *Voyages*, viii, 39. In the *Waki'at-i-Jahangiri* the date of this event is 11th Shawwāl, 1026 H. Vide *Elliot*, vi, 351.

[2] In the *Memoirs* (*Rogers and Beveridge*, ii, 399–401) the event is narrated thus: 'On Mubarak-shamba (Thursday), the 10th of the month, my son Shāh Jahān produced his own offerings—jewels and jewelled articles, fine cloths, and other rare specimens. These were all laid out in the courtyard of the *jharoka*, and arranged together with the horses and elephants adorned with gold and silver trappings. In order to please him I came down from the *jharoka* and looked through them in detail. Among all these there was a fine ruby they had bought for my son at the port of Goa for 200,000 rupees; its weight was 19⅛ tanks, or 17 miskals, and 5½ surkhs. There was no ruby in my establishment over 12 tanks, and the jewellers agreed to this valuation. Another was a sapphire, among the offerings of 'Ādil Khān; it weighed 6 tanks and 7 surkhs and was valued at 100,000 rupees. I never before saw a sapphire of such a size and good colour. Another was the Chamkora diamond, also of 'Ādil Khān's; its weight was 1 tank and 6 surkhs, which they valued at 40,000 rupees. The name of Chamkora is derived from this, that there is in the Deccan a plant called *sag-i-Chamkora*. At the time when Murtaḍa Niẓām-ul-Mulk conquered Berar he went one day with his ladies round to look at the garden, when one of the women found the diamond in a chamkora vegetable, and took it to Niẓām-ul-Mulk. From that day it became known as the Chamkora diamond, and came into the possession of the present Ibrāhīm 'Ādil Khān during the interregnum (*fatarat*) of Ahmadnagar. Another was an emerald, also among 'Ādil Khān's offerings. Although it is from a new mine, it is of such a beautiful and delicate colour as I had never before seen. Again, there were two pearls, one of the weight of 64 surkhs, or 2 miskals and 11 surkhs, and it was valued at 25,000 rupees. The other weighed 16 surkhs, and was remarkable for its round shape and exquisite delicacy. It was valued at 12,000 rupees. Another was a diamond from the offerings of Quṭb-ul-Mulk, in weight 1 tank, and valued at 30,000 rupees. There were 150 elephants, out of

moned to the court; but he preferred to stay at Mandū until he had passed the rainy season there.[1]

There is no record of Aurangzeb having visited Mandū; but his reign is commemorated by an inscription which is carved on a gateway, built at the verge of the Malwa plateau, where it suddenly dips into the valley which girdles the Mandū Fort.[2]

In the decline which set in in the Mughal empire after the death of Aurangzeb, the Marathas made several incursions into Malwa, and in A.D. 1732 Malhar Rāo Holkar led an army against Diya Bahādur, the Mughal Governor of Mandū, who was defeated and slain at

which three had gold trappings, chains, &c., and nine had silver trappings. Though twenty elephants were put into my private stud, five were very large and celebrated. The first, Nūr-Bakht, which my son presented on the day of meeting, was worth 125,000 rupees. The second, Mahīpatī, from the offerings of 'Ādil Khān, was valued at 100,000 rupees. I gave it the name of Durjansāl. Another, also from his offerings, was Bakht-Baland, and valued at 100,000 rupees; I called it Girān-bar. Another was Quddūs Khān, and the fifth was Imām Riḍa. They were from the offerings of Quṭb-ul-Mulk. Each of the two was valued at 100,000 rupees. Again, there were 100 Arab and Iraq horses, most of which were good horses. Of these, three had jewelled saddles. If the private offerings of my son and those of the rulers of the Deccan were to be written down in detail, it would be too long a business. What I accepted of his presents was worth 2,000,000 rupees. In addition to this he gave his (step-)mother, Nūr Jahān Begam, offerings worth 20,000 rupees, and 60,000 rupees to his other mothers and the Begams. Altogether my son's offerings came to 2,260,000 rupees, or 75,000 *tumāns* of the currency of Iran or 6,780,000 current Turan-khanis. Such offerings had never been made during this dynasty. I showed him much attention and favour, in fact, he is a son who is worthy of grace and kindness. I am very pleased and satisfied with him. May God Almighty allow him to enjoy long life and prosperity!'

[1] *Elliot*, vi, 383–4.

[2] *Epigraphia Indo-Moslemica*, 1909–10, p. 20.

Tīrla, a town six miles west of Dhār. As neither the next governor, Muḥammad Khān Bangash, nor his successor, Raja Jai Sing, was able to oust the Marathas, their success was admitted in A.D. 1734 by the appointment of Peshwa Bājī Rāo to be the governor of Malwa. The Peshwa, on his appointment, chose Anand Rāo Puār as his deputy. The latter settled at Dhār, the old capital of Paramāras, and since A.D. 1734 Mandū has continued to be part of the territory of the Puārs of Dhār.[1] As this family claims itself to be the descendant of the early Paramāra rulers of Malwa, Malcolm has appropriately observed: 'It is a strange coincidence that the success of the Marathas should by making Dhār the capital of Anand Rāo Puār and his descendants restore the sovereignty to a race which had seven centuries before been expelled from the government of the city and territory.'[2]

[1] Malcolm's *Central India*, pp. 78 ff.

[2] *Ibid.*

CHAPTER III

Monuments

PASSING beyond the picturesque village of Nalcha, which is situated midway between Dhār and Mandū, the visitor will notice the country on either side of the road to be thickly covered with lofty trees and tangled bush, interspersed only here and there by some crumbling tombs, the silent memorials of the heroes who shed their blood to conquer the giant fortress. The dark weather-tinted battlements break upon the view from a long distance, and as the visitor approaches near the Fort, the deep chasm of the *Kākra Koh* strikes him at once with awe and wonder. This superb ravine encircles the Mandū hill on the east and west, and slopes down towards the south in the Nimar plain; but on the north it is not very steep, and the builders of the Fort have set up a long line of arched parapets at the crest of the hill, and also built gateways and bastions at various vulnerable points.

Between the fifth and sixth furlong-stones of the twenty-first mile from Dhār, the road passes down the ravine, which is not very deep there, and a gate with a barbican has been built for the defence of the Fort.

'Ālamgīr Darwāzah

This gate is styled the 'Ālamgīr Darwāzah on account of an inscription which is carved on a tablet, fixed into a side wall of the building, mentioning that it was rebuilt during the reign of 'Ālamgīr.[1]

[1] The inscription may be translated thus:
Line 1 'During the reign of King 'Ālamgīr, the monarch of the world, this lofty gate was built anew.'

The barbican in front of the gate consists of a walled enclosure with two square bastions built at each end of the wall. The gate is arched, and the height of the building, from the present road-level to the top of the *kangūras*, is 34 feet. The covered passage measures 31 feet in length and 13 feet in width, and there are four arches, the three inner of which support a barrel-shaped roof. The outermost portion of the building has a flat roof, having been covered with slabs.

The architecture of the gate is rather plain, except for a band of carved masonry along the piers of the outer arch of somewhat conventional type.

Bhangī Darwāzah

Proceeding farther from the 'Ālamgīr Darwāzah, the visitor will pass along a stone causeway over another defile which again is not very steep, and he will notice ramparts and a second gateway built there. This is styled the Bhangī Darwāzah or 'Sweeper's Gateway'; and the story told to account for the name is that at the completion of the Fort a sweeper was immolated. The village people to this day point to a stone in the wall, within a few yards of the gateway, behind which the *Bhangī* was offered as a sacrifice to appease the gods.

The gateway is built in the pillar-and-lintel style, and is probably of Hindu times. The roof of the building has fallen down. The ascent from this gateway is steep, and large steps begin, sixty of which bring the visitor

Line 2 'It was commenced and also completed under the supervision of the exalted Khān, Muḥammad Beg Khān, in the year 1079 H. (A.D. 1668–9).'

Line 3 'Since the accession of the emperor of the world, Aurangzeb, it was the eleventh year, in writing as well as in speech.'

I. DELHI DARWĀZAH

to the Delhi Gate, the principal entrance to the Fort. The road from near the Bhangī Darwāzah makes a detour, and passes through two other gateways, styled the Gāṛī and Khirkī Darwāzahs respectively.

The steps leading to the Delhi Darwāzah consist of spacious stages, each about 18 feet from side to side and 6 to 7 feet wide; through age they are well worn and in some places disarranged.

Delhi Darwāzah

The gateway has suffered much through the rage of besiegers at various times; but the portions which are intact show a vigorous style of architecture combined with beauty of detail and grace of finish. The upper part of the outer arch, which must have been a grand structure, has fallen down; only the piers are standing. Below the former, there is a lower arch, of very fine proportions, the span being 13 feet 3 inches, and the height from the pavement 28 feet. The arch is built of a reddish stone,[1] and is beautifully crenellated along its head (Plate I). The crenellation is set with enamel tiles of a deep indigo blue, which contrasts very well with the red of the building.

The passage through the gateway was covered, but the roof has fallen down, and now unseemly buttresses of a comparatively modern date are to be noticed flanking the passage on either side. Farther up, there are three arches, which again are modern, but which show the original roof-level. Beyond these arches is the inner gate, which is of the same design as the outer one. The covered passage originally continued beyond this gate

[1] A variety of limestone with diffused red clay, containing oxide of iron.

as well, and rooms for the accommodation of guards were built on either side. The roof of the passage has fallen down, but the remains of the arches which supported it may be traced. They do not betray that lack of a sense of proportion which is shown by the three later arches referred to above.

Inside the gateway, on the west wall, the effigies of two elephants with a lotus bud and a *chakram* between may be seen. They have been executed in plaster, and are quite modern, being the emblem of the Dhār State at the present day. Below them, the figures of two peacocks are also worked out.

Coming out of the gateway, the visitor will notice on his right (west) the small low enclosure of a mosque, bearing an inscription.[1] It is an insignificant structure, built of the remains of Hindu temples and comprising a double hall (35 feet by 15 feet 6 inches) and an open court (36 feet 6 inches by 17 feet 8 inches). The openings of the hall are in the trabeate style, but the niches in the western wall are arched, and the middle one has recently been restored. The building, though having no architectural pretensions, is interesting as a memento of a period when at Mandū, except the fortifications of the Fort and the Mosque of Dilāwar Khān, few buildings had been erected, and the garrison, for emergency's sake, built such structures.

Proceeding a little farther from the Delhi Gate, the road bifurcates; one branch goes to the Royal Enclave (which will be described later), while the other goes to

[1] The inscription mentions the titles Ḥusam-ud-Dunya wad-Dīn, and also the date 28th Rabi' II, 820 H., which correspond with the title and period of Hoshang's reign (1405–32). For the text of the inscription please refer to the *Epigraphia Indo-Moslemica*, 1911–12, p. 10; but there the date has not been deciphered correctly—it should be 820 H. and not 920 H. as given.

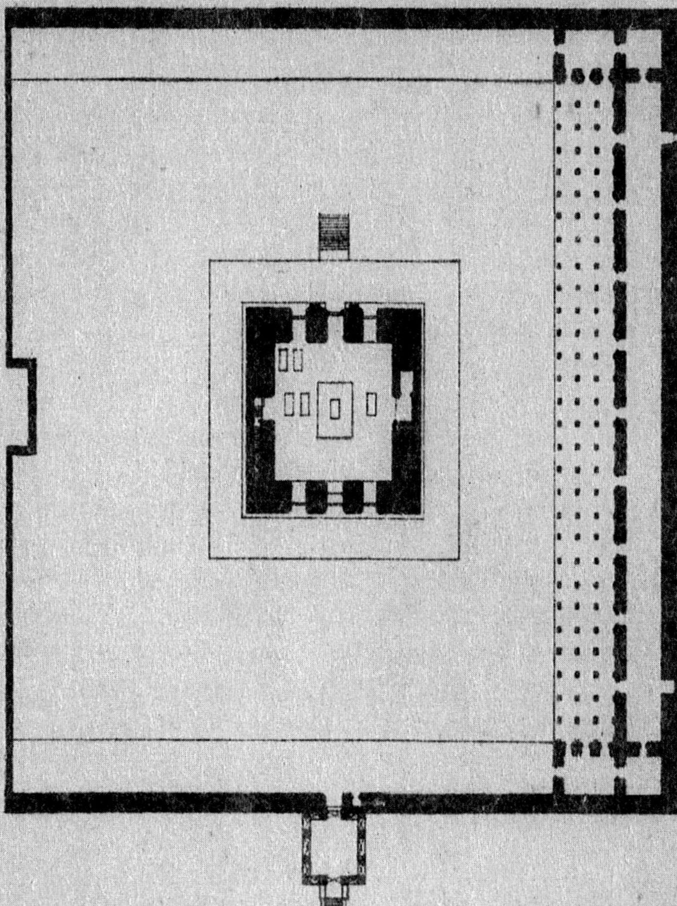

II. HOSHANG'S TOMB
Scale 80 ft. to 1 in.

the village of Mandū, where the great Mosque of Hoshang and his Tomb are situated (Map). The latter, being slightly the earlier in date, will be discussed first.

Tomb of Hoshang

The main entrance to this tomb lies towards the north, and comprises a porch crowned by a marble dome of exquisite shape. Six easy steps (each 6 inches high) lead to the pavement of the porch, which measures 18 feet 6 inches square internally. There are three arched openings in each of the sides of the porch towards the north, east, and west, the middle ones being of wider span than the side ones. The form of the arches is very becoming, and the diversity produced by the difference in their span looks very artistic. The inner square plan of the porch has been changed above into an octagon, by arches at the corners; and, a little higher, into a sixteen-sided figure by squinches, upon which the ring of the dome rests. The pillars supporting the arches have plain square shafts, and there is no ornamentation in the interior of the porch except a band of carved miniature arches set with blue ornamental tiles. On the exterior of the dome as well, the decoration is very simple, consisting of an imitation parapet carved in relief along the drum, and below it a band of stars cut in the masonry. There is also a neat device along the base of the dome, consisting of deftly-arranged leaves.

Proceeding inward from the porch, the visitor will first cross a pavement extending nearly 220 feet along the wall and 18 feet broad, entirely faced with red sandstone. On descending two steps, he will enter the court of the mausoleum, which is 227 feet 3 inches in length and 219 feet 6 inches in breadth. There is a pavement, corresponding to the one adjoining the porch, at the farther end (south) of the court, its dimensions being the same as those of the former pavement (Plate II).

The mausoleum itself is built in the middle of the court on a square marble platform, which rises 6½ feet above the ground and measures nearly 100 feet each way at the top. The sides of the platform have a carved ornamental border with projecting lobes, apparently the work of Hindu sculptors employed for the building of the tomb. The ascent to the platform is from the south, and thirteen steps lead the visitor to the pavement, which has a clear space of 14 feet on all four sides of the tomb (Plate III).

The walls of the tomb rise to a height of 31 feet 6 inches above the platform, and their surface is diversified, first by a stylobate (2 feet 6 inches high), and higher up by horizontal bands of masonry and by a *chhajja* with elephant-tusk brackets of rather wooden style. Above the *chhajja* there is a neat band of ornamental miniature arches carved in relief.

The entrance to the tomb is through an arched door of exquisite proportions, the carving of which is reminiscent of the chasteness of Greek ornamentation. Along the sides and on the top is a beautiful band of half-opened lotus flowers, and in the spandrels are rosettes carved in relief. Above the door is an ornamental parapet, and below that are blue enamel stars set in the masonry. On either side of the door are perforated screens of geometric design, which are also to be found in the walls towards the north, east, and west. It may be interesting to note that these screens have almost the same purpose, namely, to give a subdued light to the interior of the building, as the stained-glass windows in Gothic cathedrals; although the colour effect of the latter, quite appropriate for the glory of a place of wor-

III. HOSHANG'S TOMB : GENERAL VIEW

ship, would not have been suitable for the solemn calm of the Musalman tomb (Plate IV).

The interior of the mausoleum is a square, measuring 49 feet 2 inches each way,[1] which is transformed into an octagon by arches about 30 feet in height, thrown across at each corner to divert the weight of the dome from the walls, and higher up into a sixteen-sided figure by squinches which are built for the same purpose. These devices on the one hand are extremely ingenious from an architectural point of view, and on the other show admirable good taste in breaking the monotony of the building; they are always an attractive feature of the Musalman architecture.

Above the squinches, along the rim of the dome, are several bands of mouldings, one of which is composed of ornamental arches with a background of blue lapis-lazuli enamel. The architect's love for deep blue tiles for purposes of decoration is worthy of notice: the colour remains quite fresh to this day.

The sepulchre of Hoshang is built on a low marble pavement measuring 18 feet 4 inches by 14½ inches by 6 inches, tessellated with small squares of black and yellow stone. The sarcophagus is carved in the form of a casket with receding bands, and at the top a *Miḥrab* has been moulded, the posts of which are of Hindu design. There are several other graves below the dome, three of which have marble sarcophagi. One is of pink stone, and the remainder are finished with lime plaster. The interior of the tomb is extremely solemn; and the flight of arches and the expanse of the dome show the same loftiness of spirit and breadth of vision as we notice in Gothic cathedrals.

It is interesting to note that the architecture of Mandū

[1] The walls are 11 feet thick.

enjoyed a deservedly high reputation during the reign of Shāhjahān, and an inscription carved on the right jamb of the doorway of this tomb records that four architects of his court made a pilgrimage to Mandū in A.D. 1659 to show their reverence to the master builders of the place.[1] One of the four was Ustād Ḥāmid, closely associated with the building of the Tāj.

The external appearance of the dome is somewhat flat and heavy,[2] resembling to a great extent the domes of the Tughluq buildings of Delhi. The four small domes at the corners may not look very becoming, but their conical forms suggest the old steel helmets of Persian Guards, and their presence around the central majestic dome is not devoid of meaning. Such turrets around a central dome are, however, much improved in style in the later Musalman buildings of India; for example, in the Lodī tombs at Delhi or Sher Shāh's Tomb at Sassaram the turrets are a most pleasing feature of the architecture.

The finial fixed to the apex of the dome has a vase-like pedestal upon which rests a censer-shaped stand, surmounted by two pots placed one above the other and crowned by an orb and a crescent, the last being too small for the size of the building. Crescents crown

[1] The inscription may be translated thus: 'On the 9th of Rabī' II, 1070 H. (14 December, A.D. 1659), the humble votary Luṭfu'llāh, son of Master (Ustād) Aḥmad, Architect of Shāhjahān, Khwājah Jadū Rā'i, Master Sheo Rām and Master Ḥāmid, came to show our reverence and wrote these few words by way of record.'

At Delhi, in the vicinity of the Jāmi' Masjid, there is a lane styled after the name of Ustād Ḥāmid.

For the text of this inscription refer to the *Epigraphia Indo-Moslemica*, 1909–10, p. 23.

[2] The circumference near the drum is approximately 170 feet, and the height above the base nearly 40 feet.

IV. HOSHANG'S TOMB : INTERIOR

the finials of several monuments in the Deccan,[1] but they are more frequently to be found in Mesopotamia and Persia, and at Mandū the emblem was apparently copied direct from these countries.

The west wing of the court is occupied by a colonnade styled the *Dharmaśāla*, the architecture of which is interesting. It is 227 feet 3 inches in length, and 25 feet 6 inches in depth, being divided into three aisles by rows of pillars[2] which are of Hindu design. The ceiling is flat and divided into compartments by architraves resting on pillars. The arrangement of the roof is distinctly Hindu, and so is the style of the brackets supporting the drip-stones (the *Chhajja*) of the front of the building. At each end of this colonnade is a rectangular hall 25 feet 6 inches in length and 17 feet 10 inches in breadth. The roofs of these halls slope upwards from each side, forming a vault with four facets.

At the back of the colonnade is a long, narrow hall, 227 feet 3 inches long and 14 feet deep, the ceiling of which consists of a long barrel vault. The rear wall of this hall is 6 feet 9 inches thick, while the front one is only 3 feet 10 inches. There are side rooms at each end of the hall, which are square in plan and measure 14 feet each way.

The architecture of this back hall is massive, and in keeping with the general style of the tomb; but the colonnade in front of it seems to have been added at a later date when Hindu masons had a free hand in

[1] To wit, the Chānd Mīnar of Daulatabād and the tomb of 'Alī Barīd at Bidar; but they are of later date than the tomb of Hoshang.

[2] The base of each pillar is 1 foot 2 inches high and 1 foot 7 inches square; the shafts are 8 feet 3 inches high (the lower part, consisting of three divisions and formed of one block of stone, being 7 feet high; the upper part consisting of a circular cut piece of stone 1 foot 3 inches high); and the capitals are square.

building. The tomb of Hoshang very quickly came to be regarded as a sacred shrine, and on the anniversary of his death (*'Urs*) a great fair was held which continued up to the fifties of the last century, for both Malcolm and the 'Bombay Subaltern' have referred to it in their writings. On the day of the *'Urs*, the poor must have been feasted in large numbers, and the original barrel-roofed hall proving inadequate for their accommodation, the front pillared hall seems to have been added. It must be remembered that during the early Musalman supremacy of Malwa, the number of Musalman architects in comparison with the local master-builders would be very small, and while the former must have been engaged on royal buildings, minor works such as extensions or construction of ordinary public buildings would be entrusted to the Hindu architects. This is apparently the reason why in the Deccan, and even at Mandū itself, we find mosques and other structures built in the Hindu style, while simultaneously, or even earlier, buildings in Moslem style were being constructed. The date of the *Dharmasāla*, from the above considerations, may be fixed at any time from the last quarter of the fifteenth century to the middle of the sixteenth.

The external view of the Tomb of Hoshang suffers somewhat on account of its being built at the back of the Great Mosque.[1]

Jāmi' Masjid, or the Great Mosque

According to the inscription carved on the doorway of the Mosque, it was begun by Hoshang and completed

[1] The enclosure wall, which is faced with pink masonry, measures 273 feet 9 inches east to west, and 274 feet 6 inches north to south.

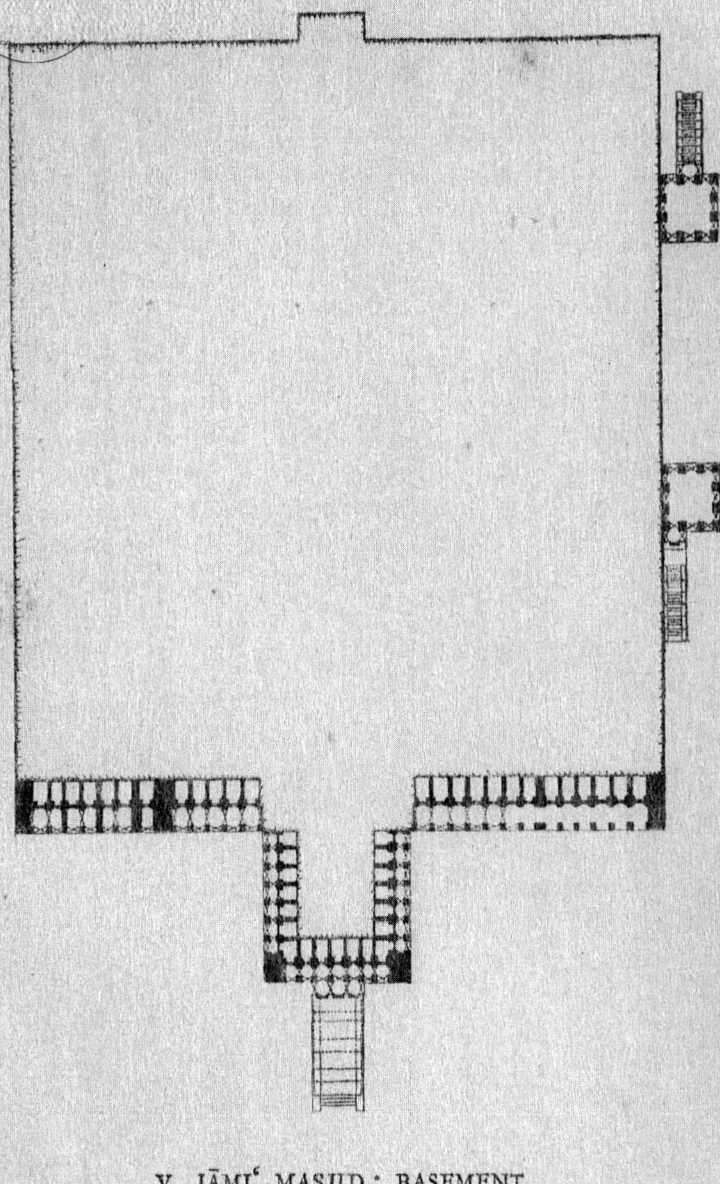

V. JĀMIʿ MASJID : BASEMENT
Scale 80 ft. to 1 in.

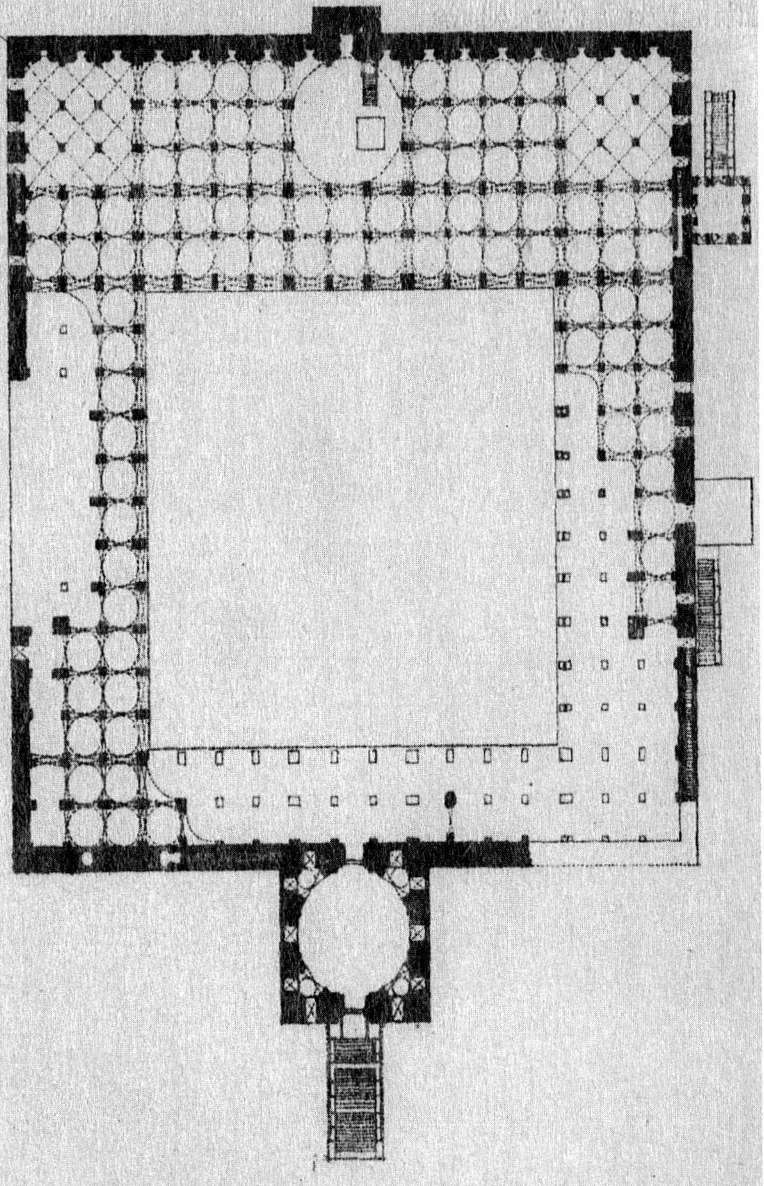

VI. JĀMIʿ MASJID
Scale 80 ft. to 1 in.

by Maḥmūd Khaljī in 858 H. (A.D. 1454).[1] The right half of the inscriptional tablet is missing, but a work entitled *Tūzuk-i-Afghānī, Armaghān-i-Shāhjahānī* (Agra lithograph, 1293 H.) gives nine out of the total eleven verses of the inscription, and, if the lines missing in the tablet are not the fabrication of the author of the *Tūzuk*, the eighth verse, declaring 'I have designed it like the Mosque of Damascus', is of considerable interest.[2] The plan of the Mosque of Mandū, however, does not correspond with that of the Mosque of Damascus, although in at least one feature the similarity is very marked, that is, in the form of the domes, which closely resemble the false wooden domes of Palestine and Syria; and the flat

[1] The text of the left half of the inscriptional tablet, which is intact, may be translated thus:

(1) 'Every pillar of its sacred enclosure is a replica of (the columns of) the Holy Abode of God (at Mecca).'

(2) . . .

(3) 'To show respect and reverence to this mosque, the angels are hovering and flying around it like the pigeons in the Sacred Enclosure (the Ka'ba).'

(4) . . .

(5) 'By the revolutions of the relentless sky when the sun of his (Hoshang's) life reached the end of horizon.'

(6) . . .

(7) 'To guard the kingdom, to complete the buildings and to repel the enemies, is my parting advice, which carry out with earnestness and full effort.'

(8) . . .

(9) 'The embodiment of Divine grace, Sultan 'Ala-ud-Dīn, the manifestation of the light of the faith and the mirror of the aspirations of people.'

(10) . . .

(11) 'According to the will of Hoshang, the latter King ('Ala-ud-Dīn) completed the building in 858 H. (A.D. 1454).'

For further particulars regarding this inscription see *Epigraphia Indo-Moslemica*, 1909–10, pp. 22–3.

[2] *Tūzuk Afghānī*, pp. 105–6.

ribs carved on the domes of the Mosque of Mandū make that similarity all the more complete. The general plan of the building rather resembles the plan of the Mosque at Kairwan, but the form of the arches is different, and in the Mosque at Mandū there is no minaret.[1] The general artistic effect of both buildings, however, is the same, and the architects seem to have been guided by common ideals.

A porch projecting nearly 55 feet from the east façade forms the main approach to the Mosque (Plates V–VI). The exterior of the building on this side is somewhat stern, and the arched openings of the small cells which were built for visitors and for the staff of the Mosque look almost like gratings in the grim walls of a fort (Plate VII). The only relieving features are a few bands of carved masonry and two borders of ornamental arches—one above the drip-stones, and the other just at the top. The latter were originally set with coloured tiles, and thus may have softened down the grimness of the building.

The cells on either side of the porch have in front of them a verandah 6 feet deep. The latter has twelve openings to the left of the steps of the porch, and thirteen to the right of them. The cells themselves measure 8 feet by 6 feet 6 inches each.

The visitor has to climb nearly thirty steps to reach the entrance to the porch, which is nearly 15 feet above the ground level. The access to the interior of the porch is arranged through a doorway with marble jambs and lintel and with exquisite carvings along its sides. Above the doorway is the outline of an arch, executed in relief; and higher up is an arched oriel of very fine proportions. There are beautiful rosettes in the spandrels, and, al-

[1] Cf. *La Mosquée de Sidi Okba Kairouan*, by H. Saladin, Plates I–VIII.

VII. JĀMIʿ MASJID : GENERAL VIEW

though the ornamentation has been done sparingly, it exhibits excellent taste. Along the sides of the arch of the oriel is a border of hollow stars, and blue tiles in small panels decorate the door in several places.

On entering through the doorway, the visitor will find himself in a spacious hall, 44 feet 8 inches square, crowned by a dome.[1] There are beautiful *jali* screens to admit light into the hall, and the interior of the building is further decorated by bands of blue enamel tiles set as stars or lozenges. The opening in the west side of the porch, leading to the court, is in the trabeate style, while an arch has been built above it, the head of which is filled with fine tracery.

Passing through the west doorway of the porch, the visitor will notice a fine panorama of arches and domes before him, the architecture of which is marked by simple beauty and vigorous character (Plate VIII). The court measures nearly 162 feet square, and there are colonnades on all four sides—those on the north and south being three aisles deep,[2] while that on the east comprises two only,[3] and that on the west as many as five.

The form of the arches and pillars is extremely graceful (Plate IX), and their arrangement is also most ingenious. The outer lines of arches along the court are double, slightly detached from each other (Plate VI). Again, the third line of arches of the western colonnade (prayer-hall) is double, and similarly the third, seventh, tenth, and fourteenth lines of that colonnade running east to west. The object in adopting this arrangement

[1] The thickness of the east wall is 9 feet, while that of the other sides is 6 feet only.

[2] Each of them is 48 feet 6 inches deep.

[3] This colonnade is 32 feet 7 inches deep.

was, first, to impart strength to the domical ceilings of all four colonnades of the building; and, further, to provide adequate support for the three large domes [1] of the western colonnade (prayer-hall), which, by this plan, have a double row of arches supporting all the four sides of their base (Plate VI). At the corners, where these double lines of arches meet, the pillars supporting them occur in clusters of four,[2] and look very picturesque. In Gothic architecture a similar effect was secured by carving delicate flutings along the sides of the otherwise gigantic columns.

The western colonnade measures 268 feet 6 inches in length and 82 feet in depth, and it is divided into a series of bays by rows of pillars which run both east to west and north to south. The pillars have no ornamentation, and consist of a base 2 feet 5 inches square and 2 feet high, and a shaft 10 feet in length. Each pillar is an angular support to the fifty-eight small domes which compose the ceiling of the colonnade. Besides these small domes, there are in this wing, as mentioned above, three large domes, the lofty and spacious interiors of which add to the dignity and beauty of the ceiling.

At each extremity of this western colonnade, below the large side domes, is an upper apartment supported by nine rather dwarfish columns. The base of each is 2 feet 6 inches square and 2 feet high, and the shaft 2 feet 10 inches. From the top of the columns arches spring diagonally, intersecting each other at their apex in the vaulted ceiling about 12 feet from the ground,

[1] They have a diameter of 42 feet inwardly.

[2] The plan given in Plate VI being on a very small scale, the bases of the pillars have been joined together, but from their dimensions the reader will be able to find where they occur in clusters of four and where in pairs.

the plan of the roof being most solid and substantial (Plate VI). One of these apartments was apparently meant for ladies, and the other for royal visitors.[1]

In the colonnade there is no ornamentation except in the western wall facing the *Qibla*, which has seventeen beautiful niches built in it. The middle of these is larger than the rest, and has several bands of exquisite carving along its sides, among which a scroll of interwoven Arabic letters containing quotations from the Holy Quran is particularly fascinating. The heads of these niches are adorned with sculptured crenellation, and the jambs are worked out in polished black stone with carvings of Hindu design. The influence of the latter style is more apparent in the pulpit, the brackets and the balustrade of which might be taken for the brackets and balustrades of many a Hindu temple of the ninth and tenth centuries (Plate X). The pulpit is eleven steps high, and has over it a canopy supported by four arches and crowned by a shapely dome of marble. It is rather rich in style, but will compare favourably with the elaborately carved wooden pulpits of North Africa or the tessellated marble pulpits of Egypt.

In view of the simple grace and plain dignity of the mosque, the elaborate carvings of the pulpit and the prayer-niche appear a little out of place; but, as indicated above, they are the work of Hindu sculptors, who have always been prone to overdo ornamentation, the preponderance of ornament over architectural forms being a salient feature of Hindu buildings.

In front of the pulpit is a small platform, 10 feet 3 inches square and 2 feet 7 inches high, which looks

[1] Such enclosures are a common feature of the Mosques at Cordova, Kairwan, and several other places in North Africa. The enclosure is styled the *Maqsūra* there.

somewhat incongruous. Apparently it is the *Mukabbar*, from which during the service the divine salutation (*Allāhu-Akbar*) was repeated for the guidance of a large congregation.

Retracing his footsteps to the court, the visitor will notice that there are, in each of the colonnades towards the court, eleven arched openings, which rise to a considerable height. Above these were rows of carved brackets supporting the drip-stones, and, higher still, a band of carved overlapping miniature arches, above which was a balustrade fixed to the top of the wall. The balustrade has decayed altogether, and its absence makes the bases of the domes of the roof rather prominent, thus detracting from the fine balance and proportion of the façade.

On the northern side of the Mosque there were two entrances, one leading to the court and the other to the right end of the prayer-hall near the *Maqsūra* (royal enclosure). Behind the latter was a porch 24 feet square, with arched openings on three sides and crowned with a dome 15 feet high, higher than the walls. This was probably the King's approach (Plate V).

A student of architecture may find interest in the

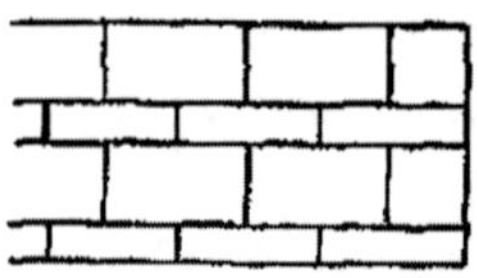

banded courses of masonry of the outer walls of the building, which have been arranged by placing the stones flat and erect alternately.

Tripoliya Gate

In front of the eastern façade of the Jāmi' Masjid, along the sides of the road, the ruins of a lofty gateway, which originally had three openings, may be noticed.[1]

1 The word '*pol*' for a gateway is quite common in Northern India and Rajputana. Students are familiar with the Hatyāpol Darwāzahs of the Agra and Delhi forts, and again with the Tripoliya gates of the latter city and of Jaipur.

VIII. JĀMIʿ MASJID : PRAYER HALL (FAÇADE)

IX. JĀMI‘ MASJID : PRAYER HALL

X. JĀMIʿ MASJID : PULPIT AND THE MIḤRĀB

Its presence near the Mosque, covering a portion of the latter, is somewhat out of keeping, and it is not unlikely that the gateway was built by some king at a later date to mark an important stage for royal processions or for the retinues of the nobles.

The gateway is built of dressed trap masonry.

The Madrasah or Ashrafī Maḥall

Facing the main gate of the Jāmi' Masjid, on the other side of the road, stands a confused mass of buildings, styled the Madrasah or the Ashrafī Maḥall.[1] The Madrasah was apparently built as an adjunct of the Great Mosque during Hoshang's reign; but later the façade and quadrangle were blocked for the basement of Maḥmūd Khaljī's tomb, and one of its corner towers expanded into the Victory Column of the same king.

The building, as it is to be seen to-day, consists of one side of a quadrangle, with a double arcade, the outer being a little narrower (8 feet 3 inches deep) than the inner (11 feet 9 inches deep). At the back of the arcades, for the accommodation of students, there are nineteen cells, the majority of them measuring 9 feet square, but some being slightly larger. The entire length of this side is 210 feet, and there were similar sides towards the north, south, and east, enclosing a spacious open court. Traces of the north and south sides can be determined by the presence of two cells in each of these directions (Plate XI).

[1] The name *Ashrafī Maḥall*, signifying 'the edifice beautiful as a gold mohur', was apparently given at a period when the people had forgotten the original name of the building. At Mandū, several old structures have been designated in this way, for example, the Chhappan Maḥall, so called on account of its having been repaired in the Saṃvat Chhappan. For a description of this building see *infra*, pp. 110–11.

The quadrangle of the Madrasah has a projection towards the west, which measures nearly 53 feet square, and has small cells (7 ft. 6 in. by 5 ft. 6 in.) built on three of its sides. There are handsome corridors (5 ft. 3 in. wide) in front of the cells, and those on the north and south sides are divided by dainty arches of very narrow span in front of each cell (Plate XI). The variety in the spans of arches, which has been noticed in the porch of Hoshang's Tomb, is much more prominent here, and adds to the beauty of the building. The ceilings of the corridors are vaulted and divided into a number of facets. Like the Jāmi' Masjid, the Madrasah is entirely built of red sandstone and again represents a style of architecture in which purity of material and grace of form are the salient features.

The projection, seen in the plan (Plate XI), extends to a distance of 30 feet 8 inches farther towards the west, and a platform marks the site of the apartment which formed the façade of the building and which was apparently demolished when Maḥmūd's tomb was built.

The Madrasah originally had a round tower at each corner of its main quadrangle, and the remains of three of them may be seen to this day at the south-west, north-west, and south-east angles of the building.

The Tower of Victory

The north-west tower of the Madrasah was later developed into a lofty column which Maḥmūd Khaljī built to commemorate his victory over Raja Kumbha of Mewar. The girth of the column is 150 feet at the base, and it rose seven storeys high, to which Jahāngīr refers in his *Memoirs*.[1] It is not known when the column

[1] *Rogers and Beveridge*, vol. ii, pp. 381–3. Finch writes of a high turret, 170 steps high. It was built of green stone like marble.

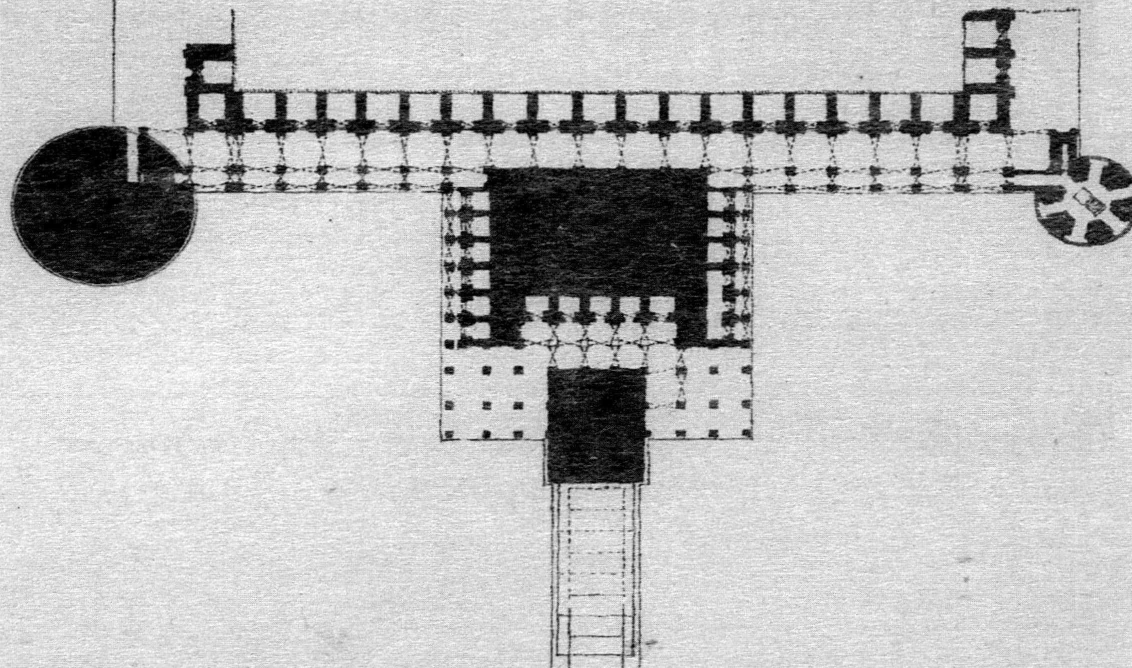

XI. ASHRAFĪ MAḤALL (MADRASAH)
Scale 64 ft. to 1 in.

XII. ASHRAFĪ MAḤALL (MADRASAH)

fell down; but only one stage of it exists now, rising to 32 feet above the ground level.

Tomb of Maḥmūd Khaljī

This mausoleum, when intact, must have been the most magnificent building at Mandū, being built entirely of marble and standing as it does on a base nearly 24 feet above the adjoining land. Seventeen broad easy steps lead the visitor to the porch, the ivory-white façade of which is relieved by bands and panels of black and yellow stone. There are three arched openings of elegant proportions on each side of the porch, the middle ones, for the sake of variety, having been built with a slightly larger span than those at the side (Plate XII).

The tomb seems to have been built in great haste, and therefore due attention was not paid to its foundations, which, as may be noticed from the disturbed level of the floor, sank under the weight of the massive walls and majestic dome, and caused the ruin of the building. The edifice was in a parlous condition in Akbar's time, and his representative, 'Imād-ud-Dīn Ḥusain, executed repairs to the building, in rather bad taste, inserting clumsy patches of red masonry in the original marble panels, and then, to take the credit to himself, so far forgot his work as to set up an inscription pronouncing that *he* built the tomb.[1]

[1] The inscription may be translated thus: 'Let it not be concealed from the spectators of this turquoise balcony that during the reign and government of His Majesty, the support of the caliphate, the shadow of God, Jalāl-ud-Dīn Muḥammad Akbar, the victorious King, this humble servant Muḥmmad Ṭāhir . . . 'Imād-ud-Dīn Ḥusain, son of Sulṭān 'Alī of Sabzwar, succeeded to *build* this lofty structure. In the month of Muḥarram 1014 H. (May, A.D. 1605).' For the text of this inscription see *Epigraphia Indo-Moslemica*, 1909–10 and 1910–11.

After the collapse of the building the debris formed a huge mound, concealing the sarcophagus of Maḥmud's grave beneath it until quite recently, when, through the instructions of Sir John Marshall, the tomb has been most carefully excavated and such of its parts as remained intact have been fully exposed. The interior of the tomb measures 65 feet 3 inches square, while the walls are 11 feet 3 inches thick. The tomb had three openings on each side, the middle being loftier than the side openings, as may be seen from the portion of the north wall still standing. The carving and calligraphic devices are of a very high order, and it appears that special Persian artists were engaged for the ornamentation of the tomb.[1]

The excavations have disclosed several graves in the sepulchral hall, the middle one being that of Maḥmūd.[2] The sarcophagus of the grave is destroyed, but its beautifully-carved yellow marble base has survived and will be admired. On the north of Maḥmūd's grave there is another with a marble sarcophagus; while on the south is a third, this last having a red stone sarcophagus (Plate XIII). Besides this, there are three other sepulchres here with red stone sarcophagi.

Standing at the middle of Maḥmūd Khaljī's tomb, one notices that the halls of Hoshang's tomb, the Jāmiʿ Masjid, and of this building are so planned that the centres of all three are in one straight line. The sepulchral hall of Maḥmūd being larger in dimensions than

[1] Calligraphic devices form an important feature of the Musalman architecture of India, and Persian artists were often engaged to design them. The names of several of these artists are preserved in contemporary inscriptions (vide *Epigraphia Indo-Moslemica*, 1915–16).

[2] He died in A.D. 1475, but the tomb must have been built during his lifetime.

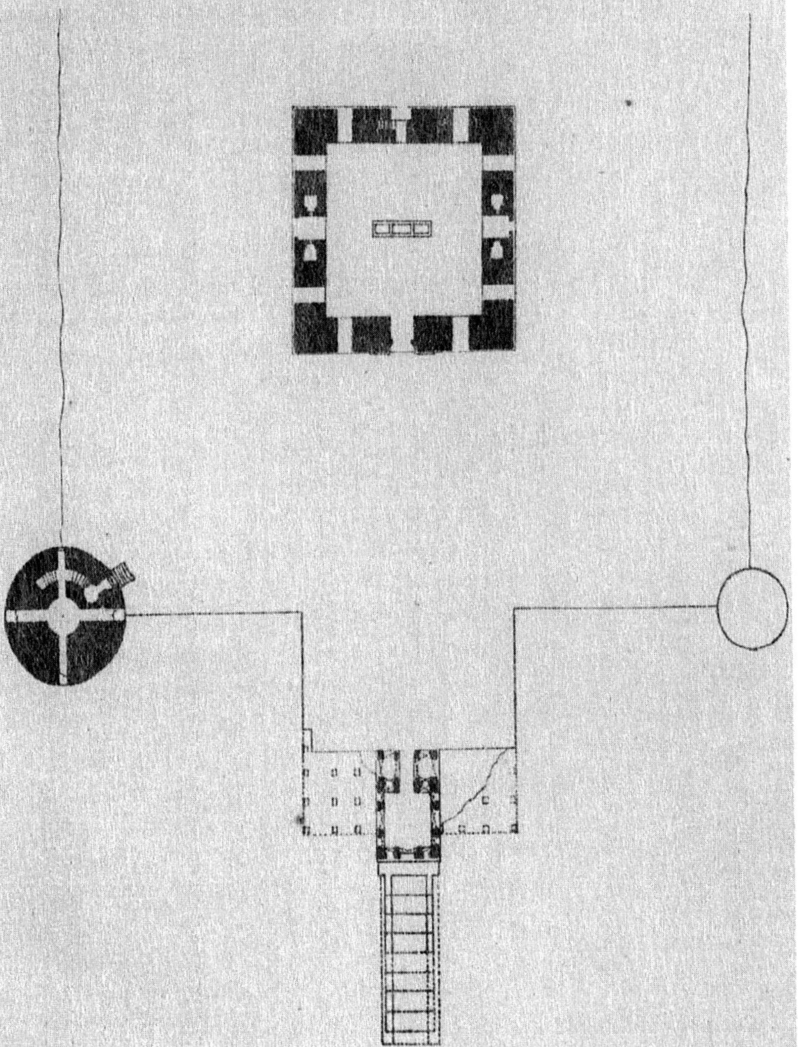

XIII. TOMB OF MAḤMŪD KHALJĪ

Scale 80 ft. to 1 in.

its two rivals, the dome crowning it must have risen higher, by at least 25 feet, than the domes of the Jāmi' Masjid and of Hoshang's tomb.

It may be interesting to note that the two principal buildings of Maḥmūd Khaljī, i.e. the Tower of Victory and the Tomb, although built on a grand scale and showing great flight of vision, did not stand the test of time, but fell within two hundred years after his demise. The stumps of marble walls, the weather-tinted carving, and the pavement of this tomb remind one of a Greek monument; and the visitor would find the charm of the place completely possessing him if he visited it shortly after sunset, when the darkening shades of evening add to the mysterious beauty of the site (Plate XIV).

Having seen this group of monuments,[1] which exhibit the 'classical' style of Mandū, the visitor may go to the Royal enclosure, wherein the 'medieval' architecture of the place is represented. The road from the Ashrafī Maḥall first skirts round the Jāmi' Masjid and Hoshang's tomb, and then goes northward until a barbican with a triple gateway is reached. The arches of the gateway will interest students of architecture, for their form is more akin to the ogee than to that of the early Ghorī and Khaljī buildings of Mandū. The gateway, from its style, seems to have been built in the latter part of the sixteenth century. On entering the Royal enclosure, the visitor will notice on his right, adjacent to the gateway, a pile of building styled the Ṭawelī Maḥall.

Ṭawelī Maḥall ✓

This is apparently a corrupt form of the Ṭawela Maḥall, meaning literally 'stables mansion', but implying

[1] Hoshang's tomb, Jāmi' Masjid, Ashrafī Maḥall, and Maḥmūd's tomb.

nothing more than 'stables block'. Its close proximity to the gateway shows that the building was the quarters of the guards, with stables on the ground floor. It has two storeys above the ground floor; and on the terrace, which commands a beautiful view of the surrounding country and ruins, there are traces of small pavilions at the south-east and south-west angles. The depth of the apartments in the various storeys differs, for each storey recedes a little behind the line of the one below.

The ground floor consists of three apartments, the outer one, probably used for stabling the horses, being wider than the two inner ones, which were meant for the housing of the grooms and for the storage of fodder. Each apartment has seven arched openings towards the north, and the roof is composed of a number of vaults.

The first storey is reached by a flight of steps, placed at the western end of the building. Like the ground floor, it also has three apartments, but the innermost here is built upon the thickness of the back wall of the former.[1] The total depth of the apartments is 47 feet, the two outer ones being each 11 feet wide, while the inner one is much wider and has a barrel-shaped ceiling supported by massive arches. Like the apartments of the ground floor, the apartments of this storey have seven arched openings towards the north, but here in front of them is an open terrace in the form of a promenade, 13 feet 8 inches wide.

Ascending another flight of steps, the visitor will reach the second storey, which has a double hall 32 feet 3 inches deep and 94 feet long. The arches supporting

[1] The back (south) wall is nearly 20 feet thick, and it would be worth investigating whether it is solid or whether there were guards' rooms on the farther (south) side of the wall, built into its thickness.

XIV. TOMB OF MAHMŪD KHALJĪ

the ceiling of the inner apartment of the hall are rather squat in appearance, their span being 13 feet while the piers are only 9 feet high[1] and the apex 11 feet 3 inches. There is an open terrace for this storey as well, measuring 14 feet 3 inches wide and extending along the entire front of the building.

Jahāz Maḥall, or the Ship Palace ✓

The visitor catches a glimpse of this picturesque edifice as soon as he enters the north gateway of the Royal enclosure, but the beauty of its refreshing environs, the lovely water-tanks begirt with trees of luxuriant foliage, can be better appreciated from the uppermost terrace of the Ṭawelī Maḥall (Plate XVII). The building has been appropriately styled the Jahāz Maḥall, i.e. the Ship Palace, for its frontage is 361 feet,[2] while its width, including the thickness of the walls, does not exceed 48 feet, and further, to complete the simile, the waters of the Kapūr Talāo (Camphor Tank) and the Munja Talāo [3] encircle it on the front (east) and the rear (west). The façade rises to a height of 31 feet 6 inches, and on the roof are built pavilions of various forms which add to the liveliness and graphic effect of the building (Plate XVI). The exact date of the construction of the palace is not known, but the joyous spirit pervading the general style of the building is very characteristic of the reign of Ghiyāth-ud-Dīn (*supra*, p. 20), and it is

[1] The piers are 4 feet 6 inches by 4 feet in thickness, and their low but massive dimensions add to the squat effect of the arches.

[2] To which may be added a projection of 26 feet 8 inches.

[3] The tank is named after the Paramāra King, Munja, who ruled at Dhār in the latter part of the tenth century.

not unlikely that he built this delightful abode for his large *harem*.

In studying the building, the visitor will notice a series of arched openings in the lower part of the façade, above which is a *chhajja* supported on stone brackets; and higher up, the wall, instead of having a stone facing, has been plastered over and decorated with small ornamental arches and with a floral motif consisting of a five-leafed pattern. The main entrance has a series of fluted bands along its arch, and contiguous to its piers are thin octagonal marble posts relieved by horizontal bands of red masonry.

Passing through the entrance, the visitor will find himself in a double hall, measuring jointly 55 feet 6 inches in length and 36 feet 6 inches in breadth (Plate XV).[1] The roof is composed of six somewhat flat vaults resting on very massive arches, the columns of which may perhaps strike him as being too thick for a hall of those dimensions. At the back of the hall, towards the west, is a beautiful pavilion projecting over the Munja Talão. It is square in plan, being 18 feet each way, but its deeply-recessed windows have made it star-shaped internally (Plate XV). The pavilion measures 28 feet square externally, and there was a gallery with a balustrade on three sides of it.[2] The ceiling is domical and decorated with a band of blue and yellow tiles.

On either side of the double hall are corridors, 36 feet 6 inches long and 12 feet 3 inches wide,[3] and beyond

[1] The thickness of the front wall is 6 feet 9 inches, while that of the back wall, in which recessed windows opening on the tank have been built, is 7 feet 6 inches.

[2] The gallery was 5 feet deep in front and 3 feet 3 inches on the other two sides.

[3] The ceilings of these corridors are barrel-shaped.

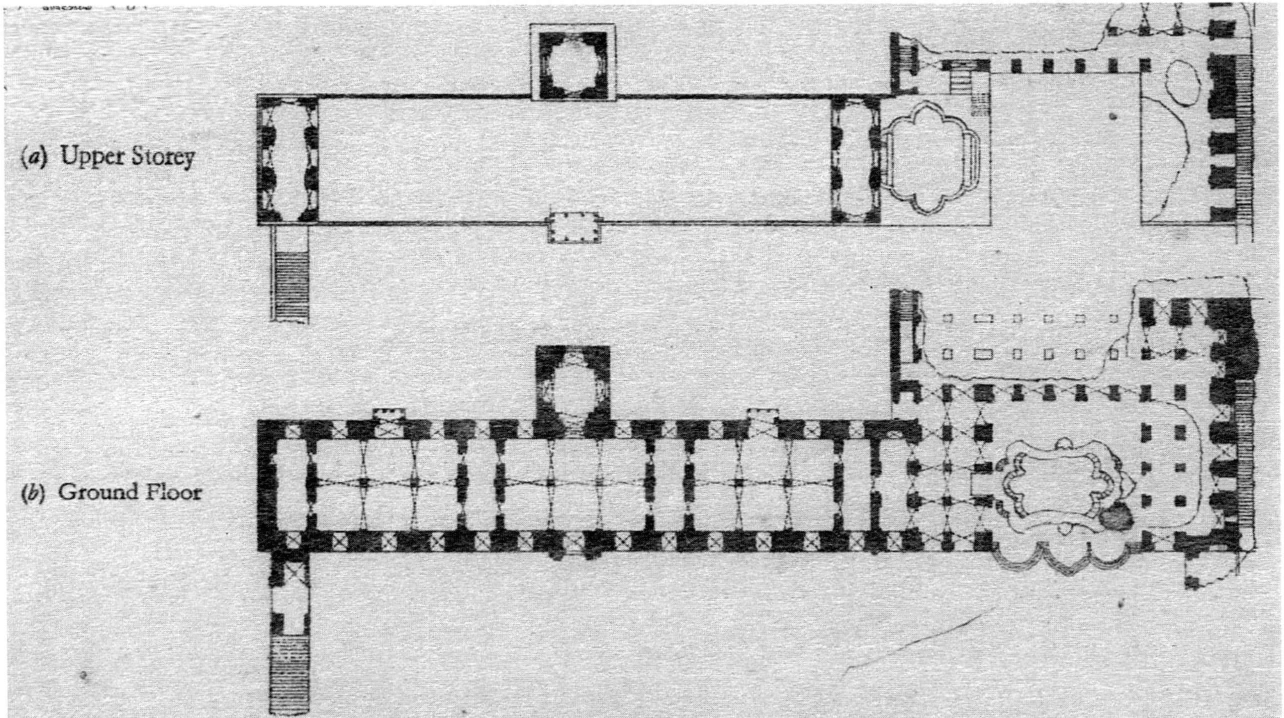

XV. JAHĀZ MAHALL (SHIP PALACE)

Scale 80 ft. to 1 in.

XVI. JAHĀZ MAḤALL : GENERAL VIEW FROM S.-E.

each of them again are replicas of the former hall. The pavilions of the latter halls, projecting over the Munja tank, are of smaller dimensions; they are rectangular in plan, projecting 5 feet from the wall, and filled with a stone framework, comprising arched and rectangular openings from which, when occupied by ladies of the *harem*, curtains might have been hung.

Beyond the replica halls, at each end (north and south) is a rectangular room 36 feet long and 10 feet 6 inches wide. The room towards the south has traces of a water-channel which seems to be connected with the aqueduct at the south end of the building. From the room on the north, a door leads to the colonnade built round a cistern of very pleasing design (Plate XV). It has an octagonal form, but the sides, instead of being flat, have been developed into arch heads. The extreme length and breadth of the cistern are 63 feet and 40 feet 3 inches respectively, and the depth in the middle is 9 feet 6 inches. For the convenience of those not knowing how to swim, there is a landing, 4 feet wide and 3 feet 9 inches below the top margin, running round the middle cavity of the cistern. The visitor can imagine the fun and revelry which would be enacted here, when in the heat of summer the ease-loving princes and princesses assembled to enjoy their bath. Wine and music might sometimes cause riots of emotion, and the reader has perhaps not forgotten the falling of King Nāṣir-ud-Dīn into the cistern in a fit of drunkenness (*supra*, pp. 24–5).

At the back of the western colonnade of the Bath there are some old steps leading to the terrace. In later times, probably during Jahāngīr's reign, a cumbersome flight of steps has been built against the front of the building at the southern end, concealing beneath it a beautiful cascade.[1] Originally there were several fountains and cascades in the court of the palace, traces of which exist to this day.

On climbing the terrace, the visitor will notice two rectangular pavilions at each end (north and south). They measure 39 feet 9 inches by 13 feet 5 inches, and have three arched openings towards the north and south, and only one towards the east and west. The ceilings of both of these halls are divided into three compartments, of which the two extreme ones are hexagonal vaults internally and in the form of a pyramid externally, while the middle one is domical both internally and externally. The architect has aimed at producing picturesqueness in the building by variety of form.

The pillars supporting the arches of the pavilions are of masonry but covered with plaster. It has been noticed above that the wall of the front of the building, above the arched openings and the *chhajja*, is also covered with plaster. This feature shows that at this period the love for stone facing, a characteristic of the early buildings of Mandū, had been lost, and the architect resorted to a pliable but less durable material for artistic effect.

The terrace measures 205 feet by 48 feet, and commands an excellent view of the plateau of Mandū and the Songarh hill. In the crimson glow of an Indian sunset, the wild beauty of the natural scenery and the panorama of domes and turrets present a spectacle perhaps not less charming than that noticeable from the Propylaeum when the venerable piles of Greek architecture are bathed in a golden light, the various hills of Athens

[1] At the back of the middle hall, to the right of the projecting pavilion, a little above the water-level, the remains of a room with two arches may be seen. These seem to be later additions to the palace.

XVII. JAHĀZ MAḤALL AND THE MUNJA TALĀO

blaze forth with a variety of colour, and the distant sea glistens like molten ore.

From the middle of the western side of the terrace a square pavilion projects which measures 18 feet 6 inches each way internally (Plate XV). It is built just above the pavilion on the ground floor. The roof is domical, and it has enamel decoration of *kangūras* [1] of five points, while above the dripstones are *kangūras* of three-pointed pattern. In the interior of the pavilion, for air and light, there are windows of rather elegant design. Their form is that of an eight-pointed star, but the points, instead of being angular, have cusped ends, except those at the top and the base, in which the cusps have the angular pointing of an arch-head. There are bands of blue and yellow tiles both inside and outside the pavilions, and also traces of paintings, the motifs of the latter being floral.

Opposite the pavilion, at the other side (east) of the terrace there is a *chhatri*, the form of which is again very becoming. It has a rectangular plan at the base, but the ceiling is hexagonal, and the outward form of the roof is pyramidal. The *chhatri* has in each side three openings of the trabeate style.

Along the front of the terrace the visitor will notice a water-channel, which starts from a water-lift built near the south-east angle of the southern pavilion and goes to the open Bath at the northern end of the roof. The Bath is similar in design to the one on the ground floor, but its dimensions are smaller, being in length 38 feet 8 inches, in breadth 37 feet 2 inches, and in depth 6 feet 10 inches. There are broad steps and landings below the top margin of the Bath, which would be utilized for rest by those who were not adepts in swimming. The

[1] *Kangūra*, literally a crenellated border.

water-channel near the south-east corner of the Bath has a highly ornamental design, and is worthy of notice.

To a student of architecture, the Jahāz Maḥall, in spite of its picturesqueness, shows a falling-off from the early style of Mandū, in which simplicity of line and vigour of design were always aimed at (Plate XVI).

Of the two tanks skirting the Jahāz Maḥall, the Kapūr Talāo is smaller.[1] Once it had masonry margins all round, and in the middle of its waters was a pavilion which was connected with the west side of the tank by a causeway. Both the pavilion and the causeway are now in a ruinous condition.

An arched underground channel connects the waters of the Kapūr Talāo with those of the Munja, which is of larger dimensions than the former, being about 750 feet square. The northern side of the Munja tank is occupied by the ruins of Royal palaces which will be described presently (Plate XVIII).

Royal Palaces and the Champa Bāolī

The forces of nature have wrought havoc most relentlessly among these luxurious retreats of the Kings of Malwa, and the visitor will notice a giant *pīpal* or a ghoulish banyan occupying the site where once stood a noble structure, and holding in its branches high in the air some fragments of the masonry of its victim. In their present state of decay it is difficult to make out the plans or lay-out of the remains; but one may form some idea of their pristine beauty and splendour by a delicately-carved pillar or an enamelled frieze which is lying tumbled in the confused mass.

To the north-west of the Jahāz Maḥall, when ap-

[1] Its western side measures nearly 450 feet.

XVIII. RUINS OF THE ROYAL PALACES

proaching these ruins, the visitor will pass by a well styled the Champa Bāolī.[1] The base of the well is approached by a subterranean passage communicating with a labyrinth of vaulted rooms, *taikhāna*, resorted to by the denizens of the Royal palaces in summer, when the glare and heat of the sun became oppressive in apartments built above the ground. These rooms are almost on a level with the water of the Munja tank, and a gallery leads to a pavilion which is built on its western bank. From the *taikhāna*, steps descend to the Bāolī, which is 18 feet square at the base. There are arched niches in the wall enclosing the Bāolī, and in front of them is a pavement, 4 feet 2 inches wide, which extends to the water. For light and air the top of the well is open, but it has been enclosed by a stone balustrade as a precaution against men or animals falling into it.

The dwelling apartments of the Kings were near the northern wall of the Royal enclosure, and stood much higher than the water-level of the Munja Talāo. At the south-east corner of an old palace, not very far from the Champa Bāolī, the remains of a *ḥammam* or hot bath will be seen. In the ceiling of this bath beautiful stars have been cut for light. Near the *ḥammam*, the ruins of several other buildings with round pillars and round marble bands may be noticed. In the early buildings of Mandū pillars are invariably square in plan, and when the round columns first came into fashion they were shaped much too thick; but in the later buildings of Ghiyāth-ud-Dīn's reign, and in those erected during his son Nāṣir-ud-Dīn's rule, they assume very elegant forms. For example, the visitor, in passing from the ruins of the

[1] Champa, a sweet-smelling flower (*Michelia champaca*), seems to be a poetic name for the well in consideration of the sweet flavour of its water.

palaces to the Water Pavilion, built near the western margin of the Munja tank, will notice near the causeway leading to the Water Pavilion some round masonry columns of colossal girth; but the marble columns of the Water Pavilion itself, which seems to be a later building, show a fine sense of proportion.

Apart from its picturesque situation, the Water Pavilion must also, from the point of view of architecture, have been a fine building once. The main façades, towards the north and east, were built of marble, artistically relieved by panels and medallions of blue and yellow tiles, some of which bear Kufic inscriptions. All that now remains of this building is a pair of halls with barrel-shaped vaulted ceilings. The star-shaped windows at the extreme end of one of these halls are worthy of notice.

In the Royal enclosure, which extends nearly 550 yards from north to south and 490 yards from east to west, the oldest building is the mosque associated with the name of Dilāwar Khān Ghorī, the first Musalman King of Malwa (*supra*, pp. 7–9). But before approaching this the visitor will pass by a massive but beautiful structure styled the Hindolā Maḥall.

Hindolā Maḥall

Hindolā in Hindi means a 'swing', and the Palace has been so styled on account of the great slope of its side walls, which make one think the building is 'swinging'. The architecture of the Hindolā Maḥall, in its simplicity and vigour, presents a strong contrast to the style of the Jahāz Maḥall, or to that of the Mosque of Malik Mughīth, which was built in A.D. 1432, during the reign of Maḥmūd Khaljī, and will be described in this book later (*infra*, pp. 82–5). The last two buildings, although indicating considerable imagination on the part of their

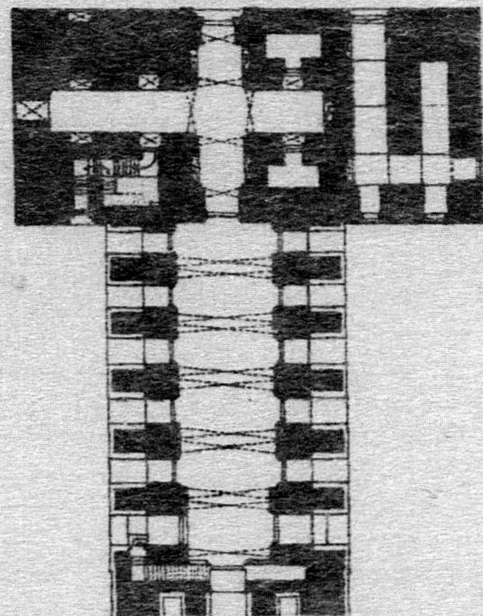

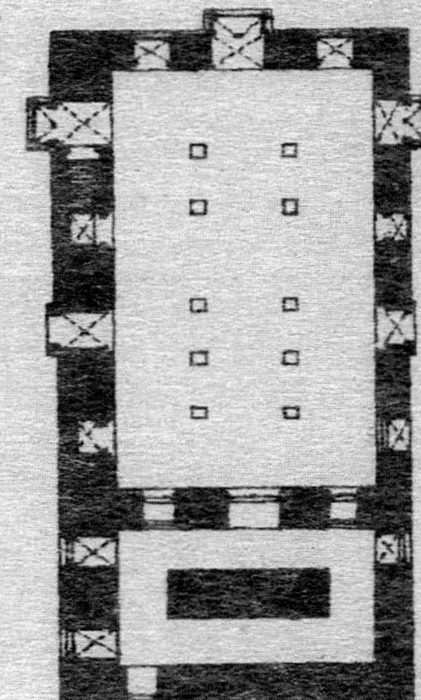

XIX. (*a*) HINDOLĀ MAHALL : GROUND PLAN
Scale 64 ft. to 1 in.

(*b*) THE SAME : UPPER STOREY
Scale 48 ft. to 1 in.

XX. HINDOLĀ MAHALL : VIEW FROM S.-E.

architects by the picturesqueness of their details, show a lack of harmony and consequent weakness in their general styles. The Hindolā Maḥall was built apparently as a protest against these buildings, and therefore its date may be fixed as somewhere near the end of Ghiyāth-ud-Dīn's reign, i.e. at the end of the fifteenth century.

The plan of the building consists of a main hall, 88 feet 5 inches long and 24 feet 8 inches wide inwardly, with a transverse projection at the north making the plan T-shaped. This seems to be a later addition, for the courses of carved masonry on the exterior of the building do not continue around the projection, but end abruptly on the sides of the hall. The entire building externally measures 156 feet long and 112 feet wide at the north end, but only 55 feet at the south end. The interior has six arched openings in each of its sides; and six double arches and one single arch supported the ceiling, which probably consisted of dish-shaped vaults[1] and, not having been properly built, has fallen down. The arch-heads of the side openings of the hall are filled with tracery of a delicate design. For light and air there are windows above the side openings of the hall, which again are filled with tracery of elegant pattern.

The east and west walls of the hall are 9 feet thick, and, to counteract the thrust of the lofty arches which supported the ceiling, the architect further strengthened them by buttresses which slope upward and project nearly 7 feet 6 inches at their base. On the exterior of the building there are only one or two bands of mouldings; but the neatly chiselled masonry with fine joints gives a very graceful appearance to the building.

The Hindolā Maḥall was probably utilized as an

[1] Cf. the flat ceiling of Ibrāhīm Ka Rauḍa at Bijapur, which is intact to this day.

Audience Hall by the King, and the T-shaped projection at the north end was built when a better-guarded approach for the Royal use became necessary. The interior of the projection has a cruciform plan, the passages from north and south and from east and west meeting in the middle (Plate XIX *a*). The ceiling of the main passage (north to south) is divided into compartments, and it seems to have been built in great haste, for the carved stones of the central compartment have been brought from some ruined early Hindu Temple and inserted without any alteration.

The projection had an upper storey for the use of the ladies, access to which was gained by two different passages. The main passage has a separate gateway towards the north, whence a flight of sloping stages, styled the *Hāthi charhāo*, lead to the upper apartments. These stages remind one of their prototypes in the minarets of Seville and Rabat, and of those, nearer India, at Cairo and Samarra.[1] At Mandū these stages were preferred to ordinary steps, apparently for the convenience of ladies, who could go up sitting in a palanquin or riding on a pony, although the name *Hāthi charhāo* indicates that an elephant could walk up the stages.

The roof of the upper storey has fallen down, but from the bases of the pillars its arrangement can be determined. There seems to have been a hall, 69 feet long and 39 feet 4 inches wide, divided into three aisles; but the interspacing between the pillars is not uniform—for example, between columns 2 and 3 from the left it is wider than between others (Plate XIX *b*). The arrangement of the pillars again does not correspond with the projecting windows in the side walls, which seem to be

[1] The passages of the minarets of Cairo and Samarra have a spiral form.

XXI. HINDOLĀ MAḤALL : VIEW FROM WEST

of an earlier date. This surmise gains strength when one notices brick and lime superstructure, which once supported the roof of the hall, but is quite incongruous in the otherwise finely chiselled masonry of the original walls of the building.[1]

The windows constitute a most picturesque feature of the building, the stern appearance of which, as noticed from the east façade, is considerably softened down on the west side by the addition of these graceful adjuncts (Plate XXI). They are rectangular in plan and crowned with a semi-pyramidal roof resembling the semi-tower of a Hindu Temple. The ladies of the *harem* would watch from them the cavalcades passing near this hall, and for their privacy the openings of the windows have been filled with trellis work of elegant pattern.[2]

[1] The earliest part of the building is the main hall, to which at a subsequent date the T-shaped projection was added. The windows of the latter are contemporaneous with it, but the hall built on its roof is decidedly of a still later period.

[2] In the Fort of Warangal is a replica of the Hindolā Maḥall, styled the *Kachaibrī* or the Hall of Justice of Shitāb Khān. The latter hall measures 86 feet by 24 feet, and its ceiling, like that of the Jahāz Maḥall, was composed of dish-shaped vaults which have fallen down. As the Hall of Shitāb Khān possesses many features in common with the Hindolā Maḥall, it is not unlikely that both were built by the same architect, or that at least the architect of the former was familiar with the last-named building. At the end of the fifteenth and beginning of the sixteenth centuries there was considerable intercourse between Malwa and the Deccan, and Shitāb Khān's Hall seems to have been constructed shortly after its prototype at Mandū was built. According to contemporary history, Shitāb Khān was Governor of Warangal under the Baihmanids at the close of the fifteenth century, but later allied himself with the Rajas of Warangal and was defeated by Sulṭān Qulī, who took possession of Warangal between A.D. 1513 and 1516. For further particulars regarding this building see *Annual Report*, Hyderabad Archaeological Department, 1925–6, pp. 11–12 and Plates XIV *b* and XV.

Dilāwar Khān's Mosque

An enclosed passage from the Hindolā Maḥall leads to the Mosque of Dilāwar Khān, which was apparently reserved for the members of the Royal Court, for the main doors of the mosque towards the east and north have no steps, while recent excavations have revealed old steps at the place where the enclosed passage from the Royal palaces ends. The mosque, according to an inscription carved on its eastern door, was built in A.D. 1405,[1] and it is the earliest dated Musalman building at Mandū. The style of architecture is, however, of a makeshift nature, and, with the exception of the niches of the prayer-hall and the eastern doorway, there is very little which may be regarded as strictly Islamic.

The plan of the building consists of a central court (96 feet by 89 feet 5 inches) enclosed by a colonnade one aisle deep (7 feet 11 inches) towards the north, east, and south, and four aisles deep towards the west, the last forming the prayer-hall or *liwan* of the mosque and measuring 105 feet 5 inches long and 32 feet 3 inches

[1] The inscription may be translated thus:

(1) 'The axis of the law of the Prophet, the support of the expanse of the Universe, high as heaven and an angel in appearance, Naṣīr-ud-Dīn, Dilāwar Khān.'

(2) 'Whose laudable deeds confirm his praiseworthy words: whose entire time is devoted to pious pursuits and worship of God.'

(3) 'He built this assembly mosque in the Fort of Mandū, which is the envy of the Holy House under the revolving dome (of the sky).'

(4) 'By the grace of the All-powerful and Compassionate this lofty structure was completed in an auspicious and opportune time during the year 808 H. (A.D. 1405–6).'

(5) 'May God protect and help him through the grace of Jesus the son of Mary and Moses the son of 'Imrān.'

XXII. HINDOLĀ MAHALL: INTERIOR

deep (Plate XXVIII *a*). The pillars of the colonnades are of various design, and show Hindu workmanship. The ceiling of the prayer-hall is also built in the Hindu style, being divided into compartments which are either star-shaped or flat.

The western wall of the prayer-hall has seven *miḥrābs*, the middle one being considerably ornamented. It has some bands of carving along the piers of its arches, while the piers themselves also are gracefully worked out in stone. The arch-head is decorated with sculptured crenellation, and the niche at the back is lined with black stone of beautiful polish.

The prayer-hall has thirteen openings towards the court, and above them is a low frieze containing a trefoil device.[1] As there are no *kangūras* along the top of the frieze, the façade of the prayer-hall looks rather incomplete.

The main door of the mosque is towards the east, and is beautifully decorated with floral scrolls and medallions. There are small entrances towards the north and south, but, as already stated, these have no steps.

The entire building measures 137 feet 1 inch by 112 feet 9 inches outwardly.[2]

Nahār Jharokā, or the Tiger Balcony

To the east of Dilawār Khān's Mosque the visitor will notice an extensive square where, during the palmy days of Mandū, the people assembled every morning to see the King. The ruins at the southern end of the square are called the Nahār Jharokā, and the King

[1] This device is frequently to be seen in the buildings of Bijapur.

[2] As the map included in this book has been drawn on a very small scale, this building is omitted therein.

showed himself to his devoted subjects from a balcony there which has recently fallen down. It was built of marble, and rested on an effigy of a tiger, hence the name Nahār Jharokā, or Tiger Balcony. It would be interesting to students of Indian history if, on the basis of this Jharokā, it could be assumed that the Musalman Kings of Malwa had adopted the ceremony of the *Darshan* even before Akbar. But the style of the buildings at the back of the Jharokā does not support this hypothesis, and it appears likely that the engineer of Jahāngīr built the balcony for the daily morning appearances of the King when he came over to stay at Mandū.[1]

The buildings at the back of the Jharokā have not yet been cleared of rank vegetation, but the visitor who ventures to enter them will find a series of rooms built in two storeys. On the ground floor there is a triple hall in the middle with two flanking halls, one each on the east and west. Each of the three apartments of the middle hall measures 21 feet by 10 feet 6 inches, while the flanking halls each measure 36 feet by 10 feet 6 inches. Beyond the latter two there is at each end a suite of three rooms measuring 10 feet 6 inches square. The ceilings of these rooms and halls consist of shallow vaults, but the niche and panel decoration of the walls and the cut plaster-work of the arches indicate that the halls were built during the Mughal period, apparently when Jahāngīr held his court at Mandū (*supra*, p. 34). The ornamentation of the rooms of the upper storey confirms this view.

A few yards to the west of the Nahār Jharokā, in the wall of the Royal enclosure, an old entrance, which is now closed, may be seen. At the rear of this entrance is

[1] Cf. the *Darshan Jharokas* of the Delhi and Agra Forts, whence the Mughal Kings showed themselves to the public every morning.

XXIII. GADĀ SHĀH'S SHOP (?)

an arcade comprising three apartments and measuring 56 feet by 35 feet jointly. The arches and pillars [1] of this building show a very fine sense of proportion; it seems to have been built by the early Kings of Mandū.

Hāthī Pol Gate

The northern gate of the Royal enclosure is styled the Hāthī Pol Gate, on account of the effigies of two elephants standing on platforms, one on either side of the gateway. The effigies are not life-size, and the trunks and backs are missing now. The legs and bellies, however, are intact and rise to a height of 5½ feet above the platforms. The figures were carved in several pieces of masonry which were joined together and afterwards plastered over. The platforms on which the effigies stand measure 25 feet 10 inches by 13 feet 6 inches, and rise 7 feet 8 inches above the ground. The walls on each side of the gateway have round bastions with stands for mounting guns.

The gateway itself consists of a pair of lofty arches built one at each end of the passage, which is covered and has a barrel-shaped roof. At each side of the passage there are small rooms for guards. The entire length of the passage between the two arches is 20 feet 4 inches, and the width 11 feet 3 inches. The form of the arches suggests that the gateway was built sometime in the sixteenth century, or even later.

Now the question arises, who built the gateway? Akbar placed the effigies of two elephants in front of the gate of the Agra Fort to commemorate his victory over the Rana of Chitor, and that gate is mentioned in

[1] The pillars consist of square shafts, 9 feet 4 inches high and 1 foot 7 inches square. Like the columns of the Jāmi' Masjid, they are fixed to square pedestals.

contemporary writings as the Hatyāpol Darwāzah. The style of the arches and the bastions of the Hatyāpol Gate of Mandū does not support the view that the latter gate might have been built by the early Kings of Malwa. The effigies themselves do not exhibit any great skill in carving, and seem to have been executed in haste. Further, Jahāngīr in his *Memoirs* has much praised his engineer for the various structures which he built for the King's residence there. For these reasons it does not seem improbable that 'Abdul Karīm, the engineer of Jahāngīr, to please the King, erected at Mandū, in imitation of the Hatyāpol Darwāzah of the Agra Fort, a similar structure, although in a less pretentious style.

Before quitting the Royal enclosure the visitor may see two old wells, styled rather poetically the Ujālā Bāolī (the Bright Well) and the Andherī Bāolī (the Dark Well). As these two, coupled with the Champā Bāolī, described above, were the only sources for the supply of drinking-water to the Palace, due care must have been taken to guard them from pollution.

Ujālā Bāolī, or the Bright Well

This is a large and deep well, and flights of steps on two sides (east and west) lead to the water-level. As this level must have changed according to seasons, in the walls enclosing the well arcades and landings have been built at various depths for the convenience of water-carriers. In the northern side of the Bāolī, at the top, is a water-lift; and corresponding to that, on the south, is a pavilion which might have been utilized by Royal guards who kept watch on the water. The rooms for guards are repeated at each stage, and thus the strictness of the watch, to which Terry has referred in his

XXIV. GADĀ SHĀH'S HOUSE (?)

account of the embassy of Sir Thomas Roe, can be appreciated.[1]

The margins of the well near the water-level measure 38 feet by 35 feet 9 inches.

Andherī Bāolī, or the Dark Well

Close by, to the south-west of the Ujālā Bāolī, is situated its rival, the Andherī Bāolī. It is so called because the corridors surrounding it and the passage leading down to the water-level, being closed above, are extremely dark. At the top, along the ground-level, there is a double-arched corridor round the well with seven openings towards the east and west and five towards the north and south.[2] On the roof of the corridors, in the middle, just above the well, is a dome with an aperture at its apex to admit light and air to the interior of the well.

From the corridors, on the ground-level, steps go down to the second stage, where a pretty arched gallery is built around the sides of the well. There is a third stage below the latter to which steps lead down, but the water often remains above that stage. The dimensions of the well near the water-level are 21 feet 10 inches square.

Gadā Shāh's Shop

The above title is a misnomer,[3] for the building, instead of being a shop, was apparently a Hall of Audience

[1] Of the scarcity of water Corryat writes: 'On the first day one of my Lord's people found a fountain which, if he had not done, he would have had to send ten *cos* every day for water to a river called Narbada. During the time of the great drought two Moor nobles daily sent ten camels to the Narbada and distributed the water to the poor.' Corryat, *Crudities*, vol. iii, Extracts (unpaged).

[2] The corridors measure 70 feet 6 inches east to west and 57 feet north to south externally.

[3] Unless the view is accepted that Gadā Shāh, or 'Beggar

built in the style of the Hindolā Maḥall, though on a much larger scale. The inner length of the building is 130 feet, and the breadth 31 feet. The roof was supported by a series of gigantic arches, two of which (30 feet 6 inches in span) still stand. To counteract the thrust of the arches, extremely massive buttresses are built along the walls, and one wonders how the hidden forces of vegetable life can muster strength sufficient to tear to pieces a colossal pile like this (Plate XXIII).

The walls of the building are faced with plaster, and bear traces of tile decoration.

The large dimensions of the hall suggest that here the King granted audience to the public (*Darbār-i-'Ām*), while the Hindolā Maḥall was reserved for select assemblies (*Darbār-i-Khāṣṣ*). The position of the two halls in relation to the Royal palaces confirms this surmise, for the Hindolā Maḥall is quite close to them, while the so-called Gadā Shāh's Shop is at a considerable distance.

Gadā Shāh's House

This house is situated to the south-west of the Gadā Shāh's Shop, but it may be approached conveniently from the road which passes in front of the Hindolā Maḥall. The building indicates the influence of Mughal architecture, and seems to have been constructed near the end of the sixteenth century or even later (Plate XXIV). It has two storeys, of which the ground apartments are now filled with debris. In the upper storey was a hall 32 feet long and 13 feet 4 inches wide, with a fountain in the middle, the surplus water from which

Master', was a nickname of Mednī Rā'i, and the hall is associated with his name. But even according to the latter view the use of the word 'shop' is far-fetched.

XXV. WALL-PAINTING IN GADĀ SHĀH'S HOUSE

XXVI. WALL-PAINTING IN GADĀ SHĀH'S HOUSE

was taken away by two spouts, one in the shape of an elephant's head and the other in that of a tiger's head. Both spouts are still intact. The ceiling of this hall had wooden beams, pieces of which may be noticed projecting from the walls in some places. At either end of the hall, towards the north and south, were small rooms measuring 13 feet by 11 feet 8 inches.

The façade of the building is decorated with ornamental panels and honeycomb designs worked out in plaster. Some geometric devices have been executed in colour. In a niche at the south-west corner of the upper hall there are two wall-paintings representing a chieftain and a lady' (Plates XXV–XXVI).[1] Who can they be? About the time of the Mughal conquest, the love stories of Bāz Bahādur and Rūpmatī filled the popular imagination. Do these paintings represent that amorous pair? The head of the male figure shows excellent modelling, and the painting must have been executed by a master artist. The colours of the figure of the lady have unfortunately faded away, but the outline of the face and the jewellery and headgear may be made out.

If the nickname Gadā Shāh should be proved to refer to Mednī Rā'i, a conjecture already hazarded in the chapter on History (*supra*, p. 28), the paintings could be taken to be those of himself and his consort.

Sāgar Talāo

Sāgar Talāo, or the Sea Tank, is a delightful expanse of clear water, girt round with stately trees and situated almost in the middle of the plateau of Mandū (Plate

[1] At the time of the author's visit they were covered with whitewash, and it was difficult to make out their detail. They have subsequently been cleaned by him, and the photographs shown in Plates XXV and XXVI taken.

XXVII). It covers an area of over 900 *bīghas*, and the water remains therein throughout the year, although in summer the other tanks of Mandū generally dry up.

The Talão has a hill towards the south, and sloping ground towards the north and west, whence it gets its water-supply during the monsoons. The original embankment is now occupied by the road which runs along the eastern side of the tank.

To the east of the tank is a picturesque group of monuments which will be described presently. There is also pleasant camping ground along the embankment, and during Christmas a large number of the European guests of the Maharaja of Dhār enjoy his hospitality in these beautiful and romantic environments. During winter the tank is frequented by a large number of ducks, which add to the attractiveness of the place; while for the lover of big-game shooting-boxes have been built by the Maharaja in the wooded dales, where to secure a panther is not extraordinary, and the lucky have often bagged a tiger.

The Mosque of Malik Mughīth

This is situated to the east of the Sāgar Talão, and, according to the inscription carved on its doorway,[1] it was built by Malik Mughīth, the father of Maḥmūd

[1] The inscription consists of seven lines of Persian verse which may be translated thus:

(1) 'Under happy omens and a lucky star, in an auspicious time and felicitous year, (i.e.) on the fourth of the Divine month (Rajab) and the great day of Friday.'

(2) 'When according to the Arab calendar 835 years and six months had passed from the *Hijrat* (Migration),'

(3) 'This place of worship of the Islam was founded in the world, the apex of the dome of which rubs its top against the dome of Heaven.'

XXVII. SĀGAR TALĀO

Khaljī, in A.D. 1432.[1] The style of architecture is hybrid, half Hindu and half Moslem, and the effect is somewhat quaint. The exterior of the building, however, does not belie its Moslem character, and at a cursory glance the arched openings of the basement, the turrets of the north-east and south-east corners of the façade, and the domes of the roof show it clearly as an Islamic structure.

The main entrance to the Mosque lies towards the east, and the visitor will first come across a porch which is nearly nine feet above the ground but is reached by twenty easy steps. On either side of the latter, in the basement of the mosque, rooms are built, which were apparently utilized for dwelling purposes by the staff of the mosque and pilgrims. There are six rooms on each side, and in front of them is an arched corridor of beautiful design. The wall above the arches has been plastered over and painted red, in imitation of the colour of the masonry with which the interior of the building is lined. The small turrets at the corners of the façade do not show much improvement in form upon the solid

(4) 'It was built by Masnad-i-'Ālī, Mughīth-ud-Dīn wad-Dunya, Ulugh-i-Ā'ẓam Humāyūn, the Khān of the seven climes and nine regions.'

(5) 'By his enterprising hand the mosque, which some style as the Abode of Safety and others believe to be the Kā'ba, came to be built.'

(6) 'The divine building was completed on the last date of the month of Shawwāl; may this good act be recorded in the Khān's *book of deeds*!'

(7) 'May Maḥmūd Shāh be praised and mentioned in the Khuṭbāh so long as mountains stand on earth and stars shine in the sky.'

It is interesting to note that the titles of Humayūn Khān given in line 4 are almost the same as given by Firishta (*supra*, p. 15). For further particulars regarding this inscription see *Epigraphia Indo-Moslemica*, 1909–10 (p. 21), and 1911–12 (p. 10).

[1] For Malik Mughīth see *supra*, pp. 13–14.

turrets of Hoshang's tomb, and, like the latter, convey a sense of heaviness.

The porch measures 24 feet by 23 feet 8 inches at the top, and it was crowned by a dome which has fallen down. The pillars supporting the dome are carved in the Hindu fashion, and may originally have belonged to some earlier building of that faith. The openings of the porch were in the pillar-and-lintel style; but for the support of the circular rim of the dome, the square plan of the porch has been transformed into an octagon by building arches across the corners (Plate XXVIII*b*), the latter serving the purpose of the squinches of an ordinary Musalman vault. The arrangement is somewhat incongruous, because the presence of a pillar just in front of an arch, as occurs here, is anything but becoming. Another anomaly to be noticed is that the interspacing between the columns supporting the arches of the octagon is not uniform, the arches facing the cardinal points having wider span than those built diagonally (Plate XXVIII*b*).

Passing through the porch, the visitor will enter a narrow colonnade 123 feet 6 inches long and only 5 feet 5 inches wide, forming the eastern side of the court of the mosque.[1] The court has similar colonnades towards the north and south, but the one towards the west (the direction in which the 'faithful' prostrate while praying) is quite wide (123 feet 9 inches by 34 feet) and divided into four aisles. These aisles are not, however, of uniform depth—the second from the *miḥrāb* is 8 feet 5 inches deep, while the remaining three are only 5 feet 5 inches.

The ceiling of the western colonnade is composed of three domes and of a number of compartments built

[1] The court itself measures 106 feet by 97 feet 2 inches.

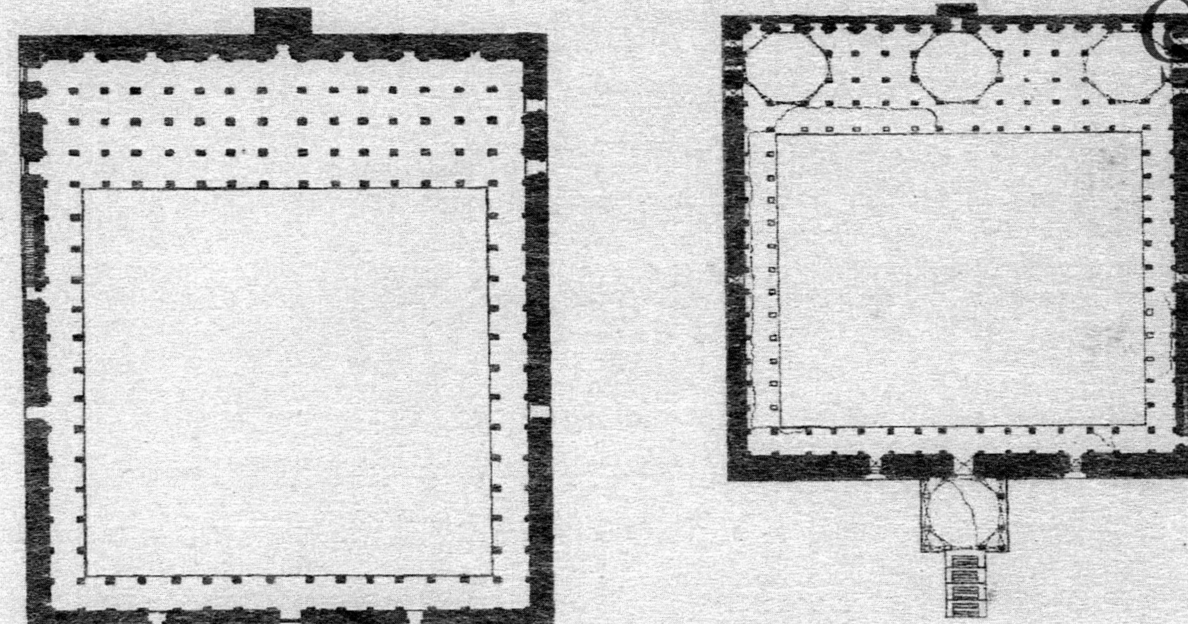

XXVIII. (*a*) MOSQUE OF DILĀWAR KHĀN
Scale 48 ft. to 1 in.

(*b*) MOSQUE OF MALIK MUGHĪTH
Scale 64 ft. to 1 in.

XXIX. MOSQUE OF MALIK MUGHĪTH

star-shaped or flat in the Hindu fashion. The slabs of the star-shaped compartments are beautifully carved. The pillars supporting the ceiling are lofty but somewhat slender, and for this reason apparently the architect has placed them at short distances from each other. The lintels above the pillars have also proved unequal to sustaining the weight of the ceiling, particularly of the domes, and have subsided in several places.

Of the three domes, one is in front of the *miḥrāb* and one each at the northern and southern ends of the colonnade. The halls below them are square in plan, but above the capitals of the pillars they become octagonal by the insertion of diagonal lintels at the four corners. Below the lintels the architect has set up imitation arches to fill the openings; but they are only ornamental, and do not sustain the weight of the domes. Like the sides of the octagonal base of the dome of the porch, the sides of the octagonal bases of these three domes are not uniform in size; and this defect, combined with the weakness of the lintels, has been the cause of the fall of the former dome, while the latter three have survived only on account of the support given to them by the ceiling of the colonnade on all four sides. The shape of the domes is somewhat flat, but resembles that of the Tughluq domes of Delhi.

In the west wall, excluding the *miḥrāb*, there are thirteen niches, seven to the right of the *miḥrāb* and six to the left. The posts and arch-heads of the niches are delicately carved, and the *miḥrāb* itself is adorned with blue tiles as well as by several bands of exquisite floral devices.

From the court, the façade of the western colonnade, besides looking squat, appears even cadaverous (Plate XXX), and discloses the fact that Hindu masons had not up to then fully mastered Musalman methods of building, and, when given a free hand, produced specimens like this.

The Caravan Sarāi

A large inn, which was apparently an adjunct of the Mosque, stands immediately in front of it and was probably constructed at the same time.

It has an extensive court, measuring 225 feet by 215 feet, along the four sides of which a series of double halls, flanked with rooms at either end, are built. The rooms seem to have been used for storing goods and valuables, while the halls were utilized for receiving the customers as well as for sleeping purposes. The ceiling of the halls is vaulted.

The plan of these inns resembles very much those of the medieval inns of Europe; but in India, on account of the hot climate, the building on each side has arched openings, while in Europe they are often closed and grated with quaint windows and door-frames. Again, in India a mosque or a temple, sometimes both, and a well or tank are necessary adjuncts of an inn. The enclosure walls of the inns in the East are always high and strong, and for the defence of merchants and their goods against highwaymen they have served the purpose of small forts.

Dā'ī Kī Chhotī Baihan Kā Maḥall

To the south of the Caravan Sarāi is a group of monuments styled the Dā'ī Kā Maḥall,[1] Dā'ī Kī Chhotī Baihan Kā Maḥall, &c., the architecture of which is well

[1] Dā'ī, 'wet-nurse'. In the *harems* of Musalman kings the selection of wet-nurses was exercised with very great care, and generally ladies of distinction were chosen for suckling the princes.

XXX. MOSQUE OF MALIK MUGHĪTH : PRAYER HALL (FAÇADE)

defined and marks the third stage in the history of the monuments of Mandū. The local masons had by that time thoroughly learned the building principles and ideals of the Musalmans, and the domes and arches do not betray such faults as have been noticed in the Mosque of Malik Mughīth, while certain features of their own crafts, especially that of wood-carving, have been most happily blended in the new style. These buildings seem to have been erected during the sixteenth century, about a century later than the Mosque of Malik Mughīth.

Proceeding from the Caravan Sarāi by a footpath, and going nearly a hundred yards towards the south, the visitor will come to the first building of the group, Dā'ī Kī Chhotī Baihan Kā Maḥall. Although styled a palace (Maḥall), it is the tomb of some lady; but among the Musalmans the houses used for dwellings during lifetime have often become the resting-places of the last remains. The tomb has a commanding situation, having been built on a double terrace, the lower part of which measures 82 feet 6 inches by 74 feet and rises 13 feet above the ground, while the upper rises 7 feet 3 inches above the former and measures nearly 35 feet square at the top (Plate XXXI).

The tomb is octagonal in plan, both externally and internally, and is crowned by a shapely dome. The latter was adorned with blue tiles, of which only traces may now be seen. For fixing the tiles on the dome, nails as well as a plaster backing have been used. The tomb is built of red chiselled masonry, and it has four arched openings facing the four cardinal points, while the remaining four sides of the octagon have been decorated with outlines of arches. The exterior of the tomb has bands of projecting masonry dividing the wall surface into panels and producing the effect of a wooden building. This feature indicates Hindu craftsmanship, and is not to be noticed in the early buildings of Mandū.

The octagonal sides of the tomb measure 19 feet 12 inches internally, and the space across is 23 feet 2 inches, which is nearly the diameter of the dome. The inner plan of the tomb, below the rim of the dome, is sixteen-sided, which has been arranged by the insertion of squinches. The decorative carvings have been sparely used, but wherever occurring they show exquisite taste.

To the west of the sepulchral hall was a small mosque, the west wall of which still exists.

Sāgarī Tank and the Garden

On the south side of the last-mentioned monument may be seen the remains of a beautiful garden and pavilion, with traces of delightful cisterns and cascades. The garden seems to have been laid out by the Mughals, for the plan of the water-channels and fountains and the decorative work of the pavilion exhibit their taste.

Dā'ī Kā Maḥall

Proceeding farther south, the Dā'ī Kā Maḥall is approached.[1] It is the most imposing structure of the group, standing on a basement nearly 16 feet high. In the western side of this basement some rooms with arched openings are built, which, as usual, were meant for the Keepers of the Tomb; and at the north-east and south-east corners, remains of circular towers may be seen, upon which, on a level with the floor of the tomb, pavilions appear to have been built.

The terrace at the top of the basement measures 92 feet 4 inches by 90 feet 8 inches, and besides the

[1] Like the previous Maḥall, it is also the tomb of a lady.

XXXI. DĀ'Ī KI CHHOTĪ BAIHAN KA MAHALL

tomb (which is built in the middle) it has a beautiful mosque at its western end. The façade and a portion of the ceiling of the mosque have fallen down, but the *Qiblah* (west) wall is intact and has some very finely carved niches. The mosque comprises a double hall (61 feet 4 inches by 28 feet 3 inches), and originally the ceiling was composed of ten vaults, seven of which, being somewhat flat, were concealed in the thickness of the roof, while the remaining three projected in a bulbous form above it. Two of the latter still exist, and internally are decorated with beautiful tiles. At the northern and southern ends of the mosque, windows of very elegant design project from the wall. They have balustrades of Hindu design, and the brackets supporting them are of the same workmanship, representing elephant tusks. The roof of the windows is in the form of a semi-pyramid, and is decorated with tiles near the base.

The tomb proper is square in plan and measures 37 feet 6 inches on each side externally and 26 feet 6 inches internally. The dome of the tomb has an elongated neck similar to those of its contemporaries in the Deccan, and the ornamental parapet with small kiosks (*guldastās*) encircling the drum, although at Mandū peculiar to this dome, is a common decorative feature of the Quṭb Shāhī domes of Golconda (Deccan). The resemblance of these architectural features is due, as is suggested before (*supra*, p. 73), to frequent intercourse between Malwa and the Deccan in the sixteenth century.

Echo Point

Having retraced his footsteps to the embankment of the Sāgar Talāo, when the visitor proceeds towards the south he will pass by a beautiful grove of trees, at which point, if he were to sing facing the Dā'ī Kā Maḥall, a very fine echo would be produced. In olden days, people resting in that charming grove after a toilsome journey up the Mandū hill, and carolling a line in lazy mood, might have been frightened by the echo, believing that in the solitude of the wood some sylvan deity was imitating them.

Farther south the road passes through many a knoll and dale covered with thick forest, but interspersed among its dense growth will be found some Bhīl huts, and children will be noticed grazing the cows and practising archery with primitive bows and arrows. On a knoll south of the Sāgar tank is a beautiful monument styled the

Jālī Maḥall (No. 1)

This is really the family vault of some noble, and contains four graves. The sepulchral hall measures inwardly 20 feet 7 inches square, and externally 33 feet. There are three arched openings in each side of the hall, and eleven of these (the exception being the middle opening on the south side) are filled with screens exquisitely carved both outside and inside. The devices worked out on the screens are chiefly geometric patterns of the Musalman style. The name Jālī Maḥall is based on these carved screens; but actually there is no *jālī* work, for the screens are not perforated. The tomb is built entirely of red stone, and is crowned with a dome the form of which is an arc of three-fourths of a circle.

Below the hill on which the Jālī Maḥall (No. 1) is perched, the road takes a turn to the east, and after going some distance in that direction bends once more to the south and passes through an enclosure which at

XXXII. DĀ'Ī KA MAḤALL

one time defended the palace and pleasure retreat associated with the name of Bāz Bahādur and his sweetheart, the well-known Rūpmatī.

Rīwā Kund

On approaching these delightful monuments, the first object to attract the eye is the Rīwā Kund, with its beautiful expanse of crystal waters reflecting like a mirror the umbrageous foliage of its banks (Plate XXXIII).[1] The Kund is lined with masonry, and flights of steps descend to the water-level, walking up and down which may always be seen lines of village women, for the waters of the tank are still sacred to the Hindu, and people from distant lands assemble here to bathe in the Kund and to carry its holy water away (Plate XXXIV). The reader perhaps has still in his recollection the romantic story about the building of the reservoir (*supra*, pp. 32–3, footnote 3); but the hill towards the south has a declivity here, and it is likely that a natural spring existed from time immemorial, the old traditions of which became associated with the name of Bāz Bahādur and Rūpmatī when they widened and rebuilt the Kund.

The dyke at the northern end of the tank is about 73 feet broad now, but there are traces of an old brick wall behind the outer masonry retaining wall, the latter apparently having been constructed subsequently to strengthen the dyke. The measurement of the Kund at this end (north) is 235 feet 6 inches, but its eastern and western sides are considerably longer. There was a water-lift at the northern end to supply the requirements

[1] At the time of the author's visit (March) the *Kohum* tree was just putting out new leaves, and it was a charming sight to see two trees entirely decked with beautiful red foliage.

of the adjoining Palace. The remains of the old aqueduct may still be seen in front of the main gateway of the Palace.

Above the north-west angle of the Kund are some halls, the remnants of the pleasure-house which once stood there. The plan and the architecture of these halls show that they are of different periods. Originally there seems to have been a double hall (77 feet 7 inches long and 31 feet wide) with five arched openings towards the water and a platform in front of it. This double hall still exists, and the span of the arches of its openings is 10 feet 10 inches. In later times, apparently, when the King resided at the adjoining Palace, living accommodation was required for his retinue, so in front of the original hall another hall with two apartments (measuring jointly 42 feet by 30 feet 8 inches) was built; but the latter covered only three arches of the façade of the former. In front of the remaining two openings of the original hall may be seen traces of a cistern. The pillars of the extension are octagonal—a form for columns then adopted at Mandū perhaps for the first time. It is interesting to note also that the sculptor's fondness for this form is traceable in the octagonal stone sockets of the original hall, which must have been inserted in the openings in order to set up doors for the partition of the two halls.

The arches of the extension hall are rather wide, being 13 feet in span, and in view of their low height they look somewhat squat.

Bāẓ Bahādur's Palace

The Palace is built on the slope of the hill to the east of the Rīwā Kund, commanding a most beautiful situation. Forty broad steps, which for further convenience

XXXIII. RĪWĀ KUND AND BĀZ BAHĀDUR'S PALACE

XXXIV. RĪWĀ KUND : VIEW FROM N.-E.

have ten landings, lead the visitor from the dyke of the Kund to the first gateway of the Palace, which faces the north. Here, above the arch of the entrance, a Persian inscription is carved, setting forth the fact that the Palace was built by Nāṣir-ud-Dīn in 914 H. (A.D. 1508). Bāz Bahādur evidently took a fancy to the Palace on account of its close proximity to the Rīwā Kund, which must have been a place of frequent pilgrimage for his lady-love, the sweet Rūpmatī. Also, during his residence he probably made considerable extensions therein; so, despite the inscription, it will not be an error to associate the building with Bāz Bahādur's name.

The gateway comprises a covered passage with an arched opening at each end. The passage is 11 feet wide, and has a vaulted roof. At each side of the passage there are rooms for the guards. These rooms are rectangular in plan, and their ceiling is composed of vaults with several facets. Passing beyond the inner arch, the passage turns towards the east, and the visitor will find a porch which gives access to the outer court of the Palace (Plate XXXV). The exterior of the building is covered with plaster, with the exception of the two entrances, which are faced with red masonry. The entrances lead to the interior of the Palace at different points.

At the northern end of this outer court there are steps which descend to the basement, wherein a series of vaulted rooms are built. The middle room is rectangular in plan and measures 46 feet 6 inches by 16 feet 2 inches. In front of it is an octagonal pavilion which projects from the building and breaks the monotony of the otherwise uniform surface of the front wall. Below the basement the ground slopes down into another stage in which once were laid out the Royal Gardens, the traces of which may be seen to this day.

For entering the principal apartments of the Palace, the visitor must return to the court and go through another gateway, from which the passage first turns to the east, afterwards towards the north, and finally again towards the east. This zigzag arrangement was preferred in order to seclude the denizens of the Palace from the public gaze.

Beyond the passage the visitor will find himself in a spacious court, with halls and rooms on all four sides and a beautiful cistern in its middle.[1] The dimensions of the court are 89 feet 5 inches by 84 feet, while the cistern measures 50 feet on each side. The apartments on the north side of the court comprise a colonnade (83 feet long, 17 feet 8 inches wide) with a room at each end (17 feet 8 inches square) and an octagonal pavilion projecting from its northern side (Plate XXXVI). The colonnade has nine arched openings towards the court, and as the width of these openings differs, the variety in the span of the arches produces a picturesque effect in the façade of the building.[2] The pavilion overlooked the gardens, which, as already mentioned, were laid out in the stage below the basement of the Palace. The octagonal form of the pavilion may remind the visitor of the Muthamman Burj of Delhi, or that of Agra; there the lovely mosaics and delicate carving give the impression of a fairy abode, but such beauties are not to be found in the somewhat plain pavilion of Mandū. The arches of the octagon are open here, but screens might

[1] The cistern received water from the Rīwā Kund by means of an aqueduct, traces of which may be seen in front of the outer gateway of the Palace and also along the south and west walls of the outer court.

[2] The arches are of three different spans, i.e. 9 feet 2 inches, 6 feet 4 inches, and 4 feet 8 inches.

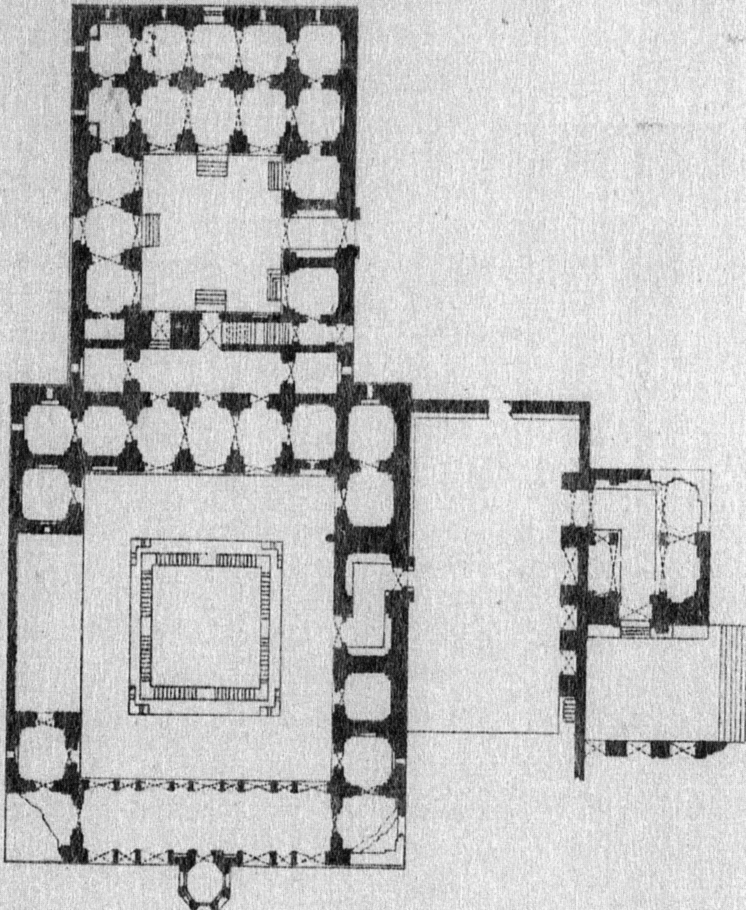

XXXV. BĀZ BAHĀDUR'S PALACE

Scale 64 ft. to 1 in.

* *Note.*—The steps extend farther towards the west, but they have not been shown here

XXXVI. BĀZ BAHĀDUR'S PALACE: NORTHERN HALL

have been hung when the ladies occupied the pavilion. The octagon measures 15 feet across.

The roofs of the colonnade and of the rooms at the eastern and western ends have fallen down. The latter probably had *Bāradarīs* [1] with domical roofs built above them, such as are to be seen on the corresponding side of the Palace.

The eastern side of the court has a square room (15 feet each side) at each end, and an open space between them (15 feet 3 inches square), the significance of which is not quite clear (Plate XXXV). That it was open originally is certain, for the parapet, the cornice, the tiles, and plinth bands of the two extreme rooms would not have been continued on their façades towards the open space if the latter had been covered. In the western side of the court, corresponding to the open space in the eastern side, is the entrance to the Palace, so the view might be taken that the open space was reserved for an entrance on this side as well. But the hill behind the enclosure of the Palace towards the east has a sharp slope, and the need of an entrance on that side is not apparent.

Corresponding to the square rooms of the east side, there are similar rooms in the west, built on either side of the entrance; they measure 15 feet 3 inches square.

The apartments on the south side of the court do not correspond with those on the north (Plate XXXVII). The main hall measures 47 feet 3 inches by 18 feet 6 inches, and it is divided into three bays by somewhat squat arches, their span being 11 feet 2 inches. The ceiling of the hall is vaulted. At each end of the hall is a pair of rooms each measuring 14 feet square (Plate

[1] *Bāradarī*, a square or rectangular pavilion with three arched openings in each of its sides.

XXXV). At the back of the hall (south) there is another of narrower depth (12 feet 4 inches). Its ceiling is flat with slight curves near the wall. The ceiling of the Hindolā Maḥall (*supra*, p. 71), which has fallen down, was also of this style. There are rooms (12 feet 4 inches square) at each end of the back hall.

An opening in the back hall leads to the steps descending to another quadrangle, which is of smaller dimensions (46 feet square) than the first court, and was apparently meant for the attendants of the Palace.

The eastern side of this quadrangle has a hall (47 feet 2 inches long and 18 feet 10 inches wide) with three arched openings. The hall towards the south has also three arched openings, but it consists of two apartments, the outer measuring 47 feet 2 inches by 19 feet 2 inches, and the inner being of the same length but slightly narrower (i.e. 14 feet 8 inches wide). The ceiling of the hall has been divided into six compartments by the insertion of arches. At either end of the hall is a pair of rooms measuring 14 feet 8 inches square.

In the western side of the quadrangle, besides the entrance (which is in the middle), there are two rooms, one at each end. They measure 18 feet 10 inches by 14 feet 2 inches uniformly.

A flight of thirty-one steps, built into the wall separating the attendants' quadrangle from the main building, leads to the terrace, which is very spacious in dimensions, and has two beautiful *Bāradarīs* built at its north-east and north-west angles. The terrace offers enchanting views of the plateau; and the visitor can imagine how in the moonlit nights of summer Bāz Bahādur would here regale himself with music, the art with which history has associated his name for all time.[1]

[1] *Supra*, p. 31.

XXXVII. BĀZ BAHĀDUR'S PALACE: SOUTHERN APARTMENTS

Apart from its picturesque situation, the Palace possesses no architectural grandeur, and belongs to the medieval period of the monuments of Mandū. The brackets supporting the drip-stones of this Palace are of the same style as those of the Jahāz Maḥall,[1] and as there are certain other features common to both, it is likely that the two are coeval, though the Jahāz Maḥall may be slightly earlier in date.[2]

Rūpmatī's Pavilions

The hill beyond Bāz Bahādur's Palace has a steep ascent, and although, through the care bestowed by the Dhār State upon the preservation of the monuments, the fair-weather road is kept motorable right to the crest of the hill, the visitor is advised to do this portion of his trek on foot.

The building seems originally to have been constructed for the purpose of watching, for the hill has a precipitous fall of nearly 1,200 feet towards the Nimar Valley, and a safer or more commanding spot could not have been selected for observing the movements of the enemy on that side.

The basement and the pavilions built on the terrace seem to have been added to the building at a later date (Plate XXXVIII). The original structure consisted of a low but massive hall (87 feet by 19 feet 10 inches) with

[1] The brackets of the pleasure-house built at the north-west angle of the Rīwā Kund are also of this style.

[2] The inner plan of the *Barādarīs* built on the roof of Bāz Bahādur's Palace is octagonal, like that of the porch of Malik Mughīth's Mosque (*supra*, p. 84); and although in the former the shape of the pillars and the dome, as well as the method of building, are much improved, the presence of pillars just in front of the diagonal arches of the octagon still appears confusing.

two rooms (each nearly 15 feet square) built at the ends, such as we see on the first stage (Plate XXXIX). The walls of the hall, like the Tughluq buildings, have a sharp slope towards the base, and the arches supporting the ceiling are also heavy in proportion (their span being 13 feet 8 inches). The hall has five arched openings on each side (east and west), while the rooms built at the ends have only one.

Above the entrance to the room, at the north end of the hall, an inscriptional tablet is built into the wall. As the letters are much abraded, the tablet was probably fixed originally into the empty niche shown in the east façade of the building, for inside the hall there appears no reason for its weathering; and further, the marginal stones around the tablet are clumsily set, and seem to have been inserted in comparatively modern times. The few words of the inscription which can be made out refer to a monastery connected with some saint of Dhār, and it is just possible that at some period in its history the building may have assumed that character, but essentially it appears to be constructed more for military purposes than for religious meditation.

The basement was added perhaps when the need of keeping a larger guard at the place was felt.[1] Its plan along the slope of the hill on which the original block is built may be understood by the diagram given here.

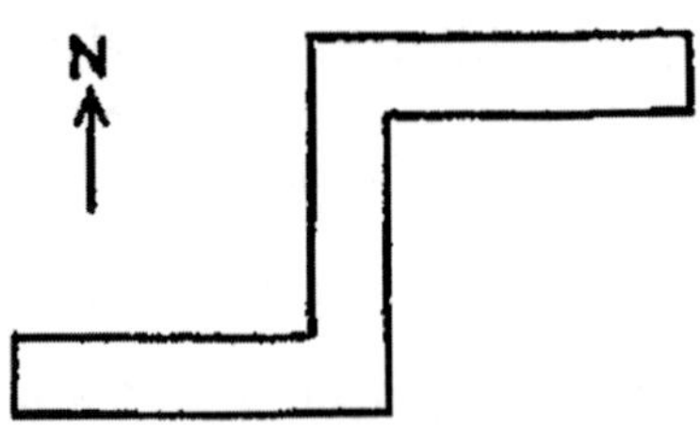

The middle portion (north to south) of the basement is built just below the western side of the original building,

[1] Or, if the inscription be trusted, when the building was utilized as a monastery.

XXXVIII. RŪPMATĪ'S PAVILIONS : VIEW FROM WEST

so that the roof of the former serves as a terrace (160 feet 4 inches by 16 feet 6 inches) in front of the latter. In the ground floor, this portion of the basement consists of a long corridor (135 feet 7 inches long and 11 feet 8 inches wide) divided across its width by a series of arches supporting a vaulted ceiling. It has also eight arched openings in its western side.

The prolongation of the basement towards the east also runs in the form of a corridor, with eleven arched openings towards the north, and a number of wide-spanned arches built across it to support the ceiling. The dimensions of this corridor are 170 feet 9 inches long and 15 feet 3 inches wide.

The projection of the basement towards the west extends to a length of 136 feet 8 inches, and is 29 feet 4 inches deep. In the interior of this projection a large cistern (measuring 81 feet 11 inches long, 13 feet 2 inches wide, and 9 feet 2 inches deep) is built, to which water came from a channel towards the east which ultimately led up to the roof, whence the waters of the monsoons were planned to flow down to the reservoir below. The height of the hill from the bed of the Narbada is, as already stated, over a thousand feet here, while the Rīwā Kund being also at some distance, the need of a reservoir for the guard stationed here must have been acutely felt. This projection has eleven arched openings towards the north.

Returning once more to the original block, the visitor will find that from the room at the south end steps lead up to the pavilions and the terrace at the top. The pavilions at their base are square in plan (16 feet 6 inches each side), but they are crowned with hemispherical domes fluted both outside and inside. The pavilions are associated with the name of Rūpmatī, who may have come for her daily *darshan* of the sacred stream of the Narbada, winding about like a white serpent in the plains below. The form of the pillars, however, which are square, and also the proportions of the arches,[1] suggest that the pavilions were built over a century earlier than Rūpmatī's time. The main hall of the building must date back to the time of Dilāwar or his son Hoshang, while the pavilions may have been built in the early part of Ghiyāth-ud-Dīn's reign, or still earlier, during Maḥmūd Khaljī's reign. The old parapet of the upper terrace shows holes for muskets, but in later times they seem to have been blocked.

To watch the sunset from the pavilions will be a novel experience in the life of the visitor; but if the nights be moonlit he should not miss paying an after-dinner visit to this romantic site, as in the solitude the enchantment of the silvery rays may perhaps roll up the curtain of Time and in fancy he may see the crumbling piles blaze forth in all their pristine glamour, gorgeous embassies waiting on the kings, justice administered in old-world fashion; nay, he may hear even the whisperings of young damsels; or, again, along the parapets he may witness fierce struggles proceeding between the besiegers and the garrison and subsequently watch troops triumphantly marching through the streets and installing a new line of kings on the throne.

Hāthī Maḥall

Between the Jāmi' Masjid and the Sāgar Talāo there is a group of monuments situated to the east of the road,

[1] There are three arches in each side of the pavilion, the middle ones being wider than those at each end. The style of the arches resembles that of the early buildings of Mandū.

XXXIX. RŪPMATĪ'S PAVILIONS: VIEW FROM N.-E.

which the visitor can easily approach from the Camping Ground (*supra*, p. 82), or from the Barnes Kothi (*infra*, p. 110), where he will probably stay during his sojourn (Map). Coming from the Camping Ground, the first building to be visited is the so-called Hāthī Maḥall, or Elephant Palace, a rather unpoetic title given to the building on account of its fat columns, resembling the legs of an elephant (Plate XL). The girth of the pillars is 12 feet 10 inches, and they certainly look disproportionate to the span or altitude of the arches which they support.[1] It has been observed before that round columns came into fashion at Mandū rather late, and to ensure the strength of the building the architect has in several places made them much too thick (*supra*, p. 69).

The plan of the building is that of a *bāradarī* (Plate XLI*a*), with twelve arched openings (three in each side) and crowned with a dome. The base of the dome externally is octagonal, and is unusually high. It is divided into three bands by masonry mouldings. Tiles seem once to have decorated these bands, for the lime bed to which they were fixed may still be seen. The *bāradarī* measures 37 feet 5 inches square, and has a grave in the middle. It would appear that the building was originally constructed as a pleasure-house, for the adjacent mosque, a necessary adjunct to a Musalman tomb, seems to have been built at a later date than the main building. The mosque is constructed much too near the latter, so spoiling its external architectural effect.

The mosque consists of a double hall, divided into ten bays by the insertion of pillars which support a vaulted ceiling. The hall has five openings towards the

1 The arches are of different spans, measuring 6 feet 5 inches and 7 feet 5 inches respectively, but their height is uniform, i.e. 13 feet 3 inches.

east; each opening containing a pair of arches supported on square masonry pillars.

Corresponding to the mosque, on the eastern side of the tomb (Plate XLI*a*) is a hall with a cistern in the middle. The roof of the hall has fallen down; but it was probably vaulted in the shape of a dish, having curves at the sides but being absolutely flat in the middle. The hall possibly served the purpose of the *khānqāh* (the abode of pilgrims) for the tomb.

From its architectural style, the building seems to have been erected towards the end of the reign of Nāṣir-ud-Dīn Khaljī, i.e. about the close of the fifteenth or the beginning of the sixteenth century.

Daryā Khān's Tomb

At a short distance to the north of the Hāthī Maḥall is another tomb, associated with the name of Daryā Khān, an official who was employed at the Royal Court of Mandū during the reign of Maḥmud II (1510–26).[1] The architecture of this monument is extremely interesting, as exhibiting the transitional stage from the style of the Jāmiʿ Masjid and Hoshang's Tomb to that of the Dā'ī Kā Maḥall and the Chhappan Maḥall.[2]

The tomb is built on a platform about 5 feet above the ground and measuring nearly 75 feet square at the top (Plate XLI*b*). The exterior of the building is faced with red masonry, and decorated tastefully with mouldings and enamel tiles—the arrangement of the latter being rather intricate, containing patterns in green, blue, light blue, yellow, and white. The presence of horizontal bands along the walls, and of octagonal posts

[1] *Supra*, p. 28. [2] *Infra*, p. 110 (Plate XLVI).

XL. HĀTHĪ MAḤALL

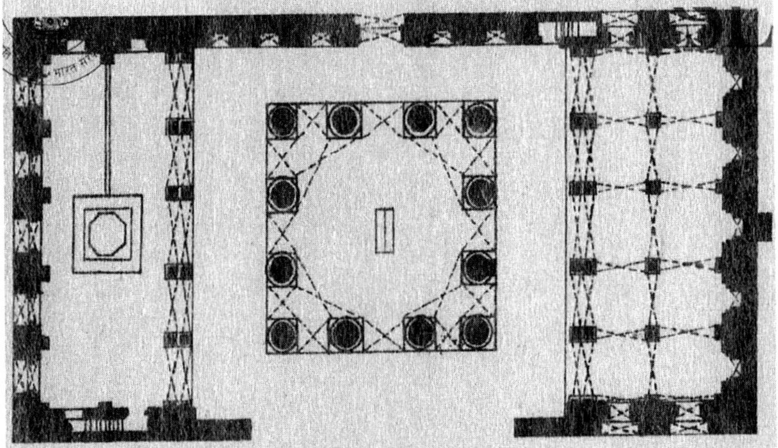

XLI. (*a*) HĀTHĪ MAHALL
Scale 32 ft. to 1 in.

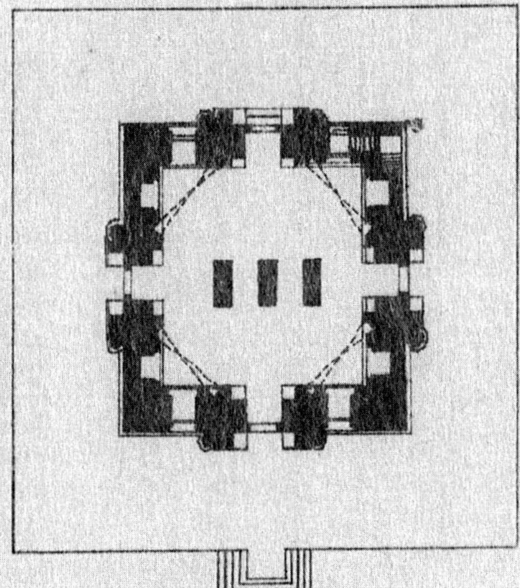

(*b*) DARYĀ KHĀN'S TOMB
Scale 32 ft. to 1 in.

near the piers of the arches, looks somewhat conventional.

The small domes at the corners of the roof are clumsy,[1] and the shape of the main dome also is not very becoming (Plate XLII). The flat ribs of plaster laid on the dome are again conventional, and apparently copied from the domes of the Jāmi' Masjid. The appearance of the dome from the interior is, however, quite shapely; and the arches built across the corners of the sepulchral hall also show a fine sense of proportion.

The sepulchral hall measures 30 feet 2 inches square, and is entered by an arched doorway facing the north. The interior has no decoration except a band of miniature arches set with deep-blue tiles. The walls, however, for purposes of light and air, are fitted with stone trellis-work of beautiful design. There are three graves, the carving on the sarcophagus of the middle one being similar to that on the sarcophagus of Maḥmūd Khaljī's grave (*supra*, p. 60).

To the west of the main building there are some vaulted halls, but they are in a ruinous condition now. One of them has a very pretty balcony hanging over the small tank on the west of the building.

The tomb is surrounded by remains of other buildings, and the visitor will notice a ruined mosque outside the enclosure towards the west; also some domes to the north, three of which are fluted like those of the Pavilions of Rūpmatī (*supra*, p. 99). The site seems to have been an important quarter, as may be judged by traces of gardens, water-channels, and pleasure-houses.

[1] They bear a close resemblance to the small domes of Hoshang's Tomb (*supra*, p. 48).

Tomb to the north of Daryā Khān's Mausoleum

This tomb has not been properly conserved as yet, but the visitor might find it worth looking into on account of its covered gallery, which is somewhat in the fashion of the circumambulatory passage round a Hindu shrine. At the corners of the gallery are fluted domes; but they are out of proportion, being much too large when compared with the size of the central dome of the tomb. In early buildings of Mandū, small domes are clustered round the main domes; but here they are built at the corners of the building, indicating an intermediate stage between the former and the domical pavilions built at the corners of buildings, such as those at Bāz Bahādur's Palace. The central apartment of the tomb measures 24 feet 3 inches, and the gallery round it is 11 feet 9 inches wide. The arches of the sepulchral hall are filled up with brick work, inserted apparently in later times when the tomb was utilized for residential purposes.

There is a mosque built in the compound of the tomb, the prayer-hall of which measures 89 feet by 36 feet 2 inches. It has nine arched openings towards the east: the fourth and sixth of them, at the north and south sides of the middle opening, are of very small size, and when repeated in the corresponding side (west) of the outer corridor of the prayer-hall they look somewhat incongruous. They were apparently planned out in order to balance the sides of the central apartment of the hall, which has two rather wide arches on each of its sides towards the north and south.

The ceiling of the prayer-hall is composed of seven domes, one of which is in the middle and three on either side towards the north and south. There are small fluted turrets at the corners of the building.

XLII. DARYĀ KHĀN'S TOMB: VIEW FROM N.-W.

XLIII. DARYĀ KHĀN'S TOMB

Mr. Henry Cousins located the site of Sir Thomas Roe's residence at Mandū near the Tārāpūr Gate,[1] where a small mosque still exists which has recently been thoroughly conserved. The mosque consists of a double hall, measuring only 36 feet by 27 feet 5 inches, and one may wonder how it would have accommodated the large party of the Ambassador. Again, it is not along the roadside, and has no apartments such as the Emperor could praise as he did when he paid a visit to Sir Thomas Roe at his residence.[2]

Some authorities have recently located it farther north along the road which goes from the Chhappan Maḥall to the Tārāpūr Gate. The remains there consist of a low masonry enclosure, and some rooms built at the western side. There are a mosque and a tomb in the vicinity, but the character of the ruins does not correspond with the descriptions of the residence as given in the account of the Embassy.[3]

Jahāngīr during his stay must have resided within the Royal enclosure, but for taking the air he would have gone to Rūpmatī's Pavilions, the site being the highest point in the Mandū plateau and commanding an excellent view of the Nimar Valley, while the various drinking bouts and feasts would have been arranged in the delightful environs of the Sāgar Talāo or the Rīwā Kund. The processional route of the Royal party, therefore, would have lain in the direction of these monuments, and it will not be rash to suggest that the residence of the Ambassador should be located some-

[1] Not far from the tank.

[2] Opposite the mosque is a mound, covering the site of some old structure (? tomb); but its dimensions are such that one cannot presume it would have been large enough to accommodate Sir Thomas's party and secure the praise of Jahāngīr.

[3] Roe in Kerr's *Voyages*, ix, 353, and Terry's *Voyage*, 228.

where in the buildings round Daryā Khān's tomb, which, on account of their accommodation as well as of their close proximity to the road and their distance from the royal residence, fit in with the description given of Sir Thomas Roe's quarters.[1]

La'l Maḥall (or Lāl Bungalow)

La'l Maḥall, the Ruby Palace, now popularly styled the Lāl Bungalow, was the summer retreat of the Malwa kings, and it is built in the heart of woods. The palace is approached by an independent road which branches from the main one between the Daryā Khān and the Jāmi' Masjid groups of monuments (Map). The palace originally had three divisions, the middle one being reserved for receptions, while the two at the sides were for dwelling in. The middle and the west divisions are enclosed by a high wall, which seems to have been largely rebuilt at some later time, as may be judged by the poor and clumsy masonry used in its construction. The gateway, however, is old, and is built of red stone.

Passing through the gateway, the visitor will find himself in an extensive court which measures 212 feet by 157 feet. The buildings which once stood here have to a large extent fallen down, and only a platform and the remains of a *bāradarī* may now be seen. The latter measures 18 feet 5 inches square at the base, which rises 3 feet 1 inch above the ground. The roof has fallen down, but it was vaulted, and the arches supporting it

1 Terry writes: 'Out of the ruins of the mosque and tomb Roe built a lodge and there he passed the rains with his "family", including beside his secretary, chaplain and cook, thirty-three Englishmen and about sixty native servants.' Terry's *Voyage*, pp. 69 and 228.

XLIV. LĀL BUNGALOW

are intact, and show a fine sense of proportion. A large well with masonry margins exists in the north-east corner of the court. The character of the walls of the enclosure has been altered by the insertion of a number of arched niches in all four sides. That they are later additions is apparent by patches of clumsy brick-work.

The western division of the palace has a separate enclosed court, measuring 127 feet 3 inches east to west, and 105 feet 11 inches north to south. The plan of the building consists of a colonnade three aisles deep (76 feet by 37 feet jointly), with a corridor (76 feet by 12 feet 5 inches) at its back and double halls (37 feet by 21 feet 6 inches) at each end (east and west). The latter halls in their turn have a pair of rooms at their southern ends, each measuring 12 feet 9 inches by 9 feet 10 inches. The rooms are so built that they are also contiguous to the eastern and western ends of the corridor at the back of the colonnade.

The colonnade has seven openings towards the court, each opening containing a pair of arches supported on square masonry columns (Plate XLIV). There is no decoration in the building, but the design of the columns and the proportion of the arches have given an air of simple grace to it. The ceiling is divided into twenty-one compartments, which are composed of hexagonal vaults. The corridor at the back of the colonnade is rather dark, and seems to have been resorted to for a siesta in the summer, when the glare of the sun in the outer apartments is disturbing.

The double halls built at each end of the colonnade are later additions, as is disclosed by an examination of their masonry as seen from the court of the middle division of the palace.

The eastern division of the palace has a triple hall, 40 feet 6 inches deep and 61 feet 3 inches long. At each end of this hall, towards the east and west, are rectangular rooms measuring 37 feet 3 inches by 12 feet 4 inches. In front of the building is a spacious platform (97 feet by 43 feet 6 inches), with a rectangular cistern in the middle. The pillars and arches of this building are of the same style as that of their prototypes in the western division of the palace. The ceiling also is of the same design, being composed of vaults with six facets. In the south wall of the hall a cascade and a channel will be noticed. The latter is built of brick, and is apparently a later addition. The façade of the building, although built of red masonry, has in recent times been whitewashed.

There is a large well with masonry margins in the north-east corner of the court. At the eastern end of this well the remains of a *ḥammām* will also be seen. There are traces of a water-channel and several cascades around the building.

Chishtī Khān's Palace

Another luxurious resort, which is of a somewhat later date (latter half of the sixteenth century?), is built at an edge of the plateau which commands a view of the valley (*Kākra Koh*) in three directions. The palace can be approached by a foot-path which branches from the main road near the Gārī Darwāzah (*supra*, p. 43) and runs eastward along the border of the plateau for a distance of nearly three furlongs until the building is reached.

The palace is much decayed, and it is difficult to determine its plan exactly (Plate XLV). The main wing, towards the south, apparently consisted of a rectangular

XLV. CHISHTĪ KHĀN'S PALACE

hall (36 feet 2 inches long and 12 feet 7 inches deep) with a room at each end, measuring 13 feet 3 inches by 12 feet 6 inches. In front of the latter at each end there are traces of another room, measuring 17 feet 6 inches by 13 feet 3 inches. In the room at the east end of the main hall the walls are decorated with tiles and painting. There is also a Persian inscription in verse, composed in a rather epicurean vein and bearing a peculiar significance in the desolation of the surroundings.

Steps from the pavilion lead down to a chamber which was apparently used as a cellar for storing wine. In line with this chamber there are some other vaulted rooms built below the main hall.

In front of the hall and its adjuncts described above there was a pleasing court, and at its northern side another series of halls and rooms. The principal hall among the latter measures 36 feet 6 inches by 12 feet 5 inches, while to the east of it is another measuring 28 feet 10 inches by 12 feet 8 inches. On the west, however, is a small room, its dimensions being 13 feet 8 inches by 12 feet 8 inches. The ceilings of the halls were vaulted, and the ornamental fluted designs, worked out in plaster, are still intact.

Bordering the court and in front of the latter halls were some more rooms, the traces of which can be made out by the remains of walls.

The palace was evidently built as a retreat for the rainy season, when the valley is clothed with magnificent verdure, and hill-streams and waterfalls add to the grandeur of the scenery.

Chhappan Maḥall

This is the tomb of a noble, and, as alluded to above,[1] has been styled Chhappan Maḥall on account of its being repaired in the Saṃvat Chhappan. The building is perhaps the best specimen of the third stage of the architecture of Mandū, which commenced in the latter part of the reign of Nāṣir-ud-Dīn and continued until the annexation of Malwa by the Mughals.[2]

The tomb is built of red sandstone and stands on a terrace which rises 13 feet above the ground and measures 132 feet square at the top. In the basement of the terrace, towards the south, rooms with arched openings will be noticed, which are built for the accommodation of servants and pilgrims. To add to the commanding position of the mausoleum, the architect has

[1] *Supra*, p. 57.

[2] The Dā'ī Kā Maḥall, the Dā'ī Kī Chhotī Baihan Kā Maḥall, and the Jalī Maḥall (No. 1), which have been noticed above, also belong to the third period. These divisions may appear arbitrary to some critics, but the architecture of the Jāmi' Masjid does not fall in with that of the Jahāz Maḥall or Malik Mughīth's Mosque; nor can the architecture of the latter two monuments be classed with that of the Chhappan Maḥall and others of this category. Again, in studying the salient features of these monuments, it cannot be ignored that the first period is characterized by the subordinate position of Hindu craftsmanship in relation to Musalman work; while in the middle period, the Hindu builder (when given a free hand) betrays his ignorance of the building methods and ideals of the Musalmans, and the immediate result is that almost simultaneously buildings with accentuated Musalman tendencies (e.g. Hindolā Maḥall) are set up. In the last stage, a mingling of the building traditions of both is to be noticed, and although the simple grace and vigour of the first period has been lost, yet there is no jarring discord between the constituent elements, such as is to be noticed in the monuments of the second period.

XLVI. CHHAPPAN MAHALL

constructed a platform 3 feet 2 inches high above the terrace, and built the tomb on it.

The general architectural effect of the building from outside is quite pleasing, and apart from an air of dignity there is considerable rhythm in it (Plate XLVI). The beautiful brackets and mouldings of the Hindu style blend happily with the spirit of the delicately carved screens of Moslem design; while the arches and vaulting of the dome show a fine sense of proportion, and betray no ignorance of architectural principles.

The sepulchral hall is entered by an arched doorway from the south, and measures 31 feet 6 inches square. The corners of the hall are filled with squinches, and above them is a band of ornamental arches set with deep-blue tiles. Higher up, contiguous to the rim of the dome, is a fringe of delicate carvings; but the decoration is on the whole very sparing, and not at discord with the solemnity of a tomb.

At the western end of the terrace there were some old rooms which, for the convenience of visitors, the Dhār State have recently fitted up in accordance with modern requirements. As the idea of this transformation emanated from Major Barnes, the rooms have been called after him, being styled the Barnes Kothi.[1]

Nīl Kanth Palace

Nīl Kanth, or Blue Throat, is an epithet of the Hindu god Siva, and originally the site must have possessed

[1] The author had the privilege of staying in the rooms and enjoying the hospitality of the Dhār State during his visit to Mandū in March 1927, which was happily synchronous with the great Hindu festival of Holī. The pent-up emotions of the Indian peasant girl find an outlet on this occasion, and one who has seen the revelry and plain amusements of the villages in Rajputana and Malwa at this time will not easily forget them.

some shrine, however insignificant, dedicated to that god, so that the name Nīl Kanth, in spite of the Moslem character of the building, has survived during the last three centuries and a half. The situation of the palace is extremely fine, having been built on a slope of the hill, at a spot from which a magnificent view of the valley below can be obtained. Emperor Jahāngīr during his stay visited the palace with the ladies of the *harem*, and he writes that it is one of the pleasantest places in the Mandū Fort.[1]

The palace is approached by the fair-weather road which goes from the Chhappan Maḥall to the Tārāpūr Gate (Map). There are traces of a tank, a short distance above the walls, whence steps descend to the palace.[2] The plan of the building consists of a court with rooms on the east, west, and south sides, the north side being open to enjoy the view of the valley. In the middle of the court there is a beautiful cistern, to which water was supplied by a channel or cascade built along the plinth of the apartments on the south side (Plate XLVII).

The rooms on the east and west sides of the court measure 17 feet 6 inches by 12 feet 4 inches, and the roof of each is in the form of a semi-dome. They have only one opening towards the court, which consists of a large arch. The floor of these rooms is higher than the court; but they are on a lower level than the apartments on the south, which, for the sake of the cascade, have been built 6 feet 6 inches above the court.

The plan of the building on the south side consists of an inner room, which is rectangular in shape and has

[1] *Supra*, p. 34.

[2] The steps are built in the west side of the palace, and they are sixty-one in number. At the head of the steps there is also a gateway.

XLVII. NĪL KANTH OR SHĀH BUDĀGH KHĀN'S PALACE

an octagonal cistern in its middle. The water in this cistern was supplied from the tank above on the plateau, and the traces of a water-channel exist on the back of the building. There is also a cascade along the south wall of this room, from which the water flowed down into the cistern. In front of this room there is another which through a large arch overlooks the court and the valley beyond. This was the principal sitting-room, and on its walls the Emperor Akbar had some inscriptions carved which mention his expeditions to Dandes (Khandesh) and the Deccan, and also contain verses which in a pathetic vein refer to the mutability of earthly pomp and glory.[1]

[1] The inscription on the right side may be translated thus: 'In the 44th year of the Ilāhī Era, corresponding to 1008 H., when the servants of His Exalted Majesty, the refuge of the world, of heaven-like court, the shadow of God, were proceeding to conquer the Deccan, they happened to pass here.'

'Till when wilt thou boast that thy mansion has reached the heaven?
They will laugh at our vainsome heart.
Come, take warning from the history of others
Before that they listen to *our* history.'

On the left side there are two inscriptions, the translation of which is given below:

(1) 'His Majesty, the shadow of God, having conquered the Deccan and the Dandes (Khandesh), marched to (North) India in 1009 H. (A.D. 1600).' Written by Nāmī.
'At dawn I noticed an owl roosting
In the balcony of Shirwan Shāh;
Plaintively it uttered this warning,
Where all that Pomp and where all that Glory?'

(2) 'In 1009 H. (A.D. 1600) His Majesty the King Akbar, having conquered Dandes (Khandesh) and the Deccan, proceeded to (North) India.' Written by Muḥammad Mā'ṣūm.

The building has two more inscriptions, one carved on the outer

The room with inscriptions measures 17 feet 6 inches by 13 feet 3 inches, and has a vaulted ceiling in the form of a semi-orb. There is a square chamber at each end of the room (towards the east and west) measuring 11 feet 2 inches on each side.

The palace is entirely built of red stone, and its architecture presents certain features which are peculiarly Mughal, e.g. the oriel-shaped apartments with lofty arches, overlooking the court, and the water-channels and fountains laid out inside the rooms, such as can be seen in a great variety of design in the palaces at Lahore, Delhi, and Agra. This building has no architectural pretension, but its style falls in well with that of the other structures of Akbar.

arch and the other on the inner. The former states that the palace was built during the reign of Akbar, and reads as follows:

Translation

'This delightful edifice was ordered to be built during the reign of the great Sulṭān, the most just and benevolent monarch, the lord of the kings of Arab and non-Arab countries, the shadow of God in both the worlds, the master of the sea and land, the hoister of the standards of holy wars and campaigns, Abu-l-Fatḥ Jalāl-ud-Dīn Muḥammad Akbar, the victorious King; may God perpetuate his Kingdom and glory.' Written by Farīdūn Ḥusain son of Ḥātimī, in the year 982 H. (A.D. 1574).

The other inscription consists of a Persian verse, and mentions the name of Shāh Budāgh Khān, who built the palace. The following is the translation:

'The whole life may well be spent over handling clay and water (i.e. building material)

(In the hope) that perchance the godly person stay here for a while.'

Written by Shāh Budāgh Khān in 982 H.

For further particulars regarding these inscriptions the reader may refer to the *Epigraphia Indo-Moslemica*, 1909–10, pp. 25–7.

Songarh

A couple of furlongs' walk, or drive in a motor if the track has not been cut up by rain, will bring the visitor from the Nīl Kanth Palace to the foot of the Songarh hill. The top of the hill resembles the hump of a camel, and appears always an impressive sight from the plateau of Mandū. The fortifications comprise a solid masonry wall towards the south and west, while in other directions the natural precipitous declivities constitute an impregnable defence. For the support of the wall, round bastions are built, some of which bear old pieces of artillery of rather clumsy construction.

Near the neck of the plateau, connecting it with the hill, stands a gateway, the architecture of which is quite modern; it is reported that the Maratha lady Maina Bā'ī rebuilt it during her residence at Mandū in the last century. The gate has an arched entrance, and at the top has two kiosks, which are built of brick and are an eyesore as contrasting with the beautiful red masonry of the upper façade of the gate. The cusped arches of these kiosks add a further incongruity in the style of the building. The effigies of a tiger and an elephant worked out in plaster may be seen on the inner face of the gateway.

The passage-way between the plateau of Mandū and the gateway of the hill seems to have been artificially formed by filling up a shallow ravine between the two. The view of the valley from the front of the gateway is marvellous, and the visitor may notice below the ruins of some tombs and of a Caravan Sarāi which may be approached from the plateau by proceeding through the Lohānī Gate (*infra*, pp. 121–22).

A bridle path leads to the summit of the hill, but the

climb is extremely stiff and at certain points dangerous. For the visitor who, in an exuberance of spirits, may undertake the climb, there comes the reward of seeing those precipitous cliffs down which King Bahādur of Gujarat had himself and his horses lowered by ropes when surrounded by the troops of Humāyūn in A.D. 1534.[1] There are also some graves and the remains of a mosque and a reservoir. One of the graves is associated with the name of Pīr Ghaib, the 'invisible saint', who helps travellers in distress by assuming human form but disappears as soon as the help is rendered.

Tārāpūr Gate

This gate stands at the south-west brink of the plateau of Mandū, facing the Tārāpūr village which nestles in the plains below.[2] The fall of the hill beyond the outer arch of the gate is very precipitous, and although there are traces of a paved path descending to the plains, it is very difficult to believe that heavy artillery or chariots could be brought up this way, for the garrison could easily have crushed them by rolling down heavy stones. History, however, records that the Fort was invaded several times from this direction, and Humāyūn's troops are said to have scaled the walls at some point near this gateway—no insignificant feat of gallantry when it is remembered that the height of the hill here is over a thousand feet.

The plan of the gateway embraces an outer arch, whence broad masonry steps, defended on both sides by massive walls, lead first towards the west and then towards the north until a landing is reached, where

[1] *Supra*, p. 28.

[2] The visitor can approach the Gate by a cart-track, which is also motorable during winter and summer, from the Chhappan Maḥall.

XLVIII. TĀRĀPŪR GATE

Akbar ordered a gate to be built facing the west. An inscription is carved on the side wall of the gate, recording the fact that the approach to the Fort was improved by the Emperor's agent Muḥammad Ḥusain in the year 1014 H. (A.D. 1605).[1] There is no doubt that for the purpose of the Royal entry, Akbar's Gate is a distinct improvement upon the previous approach, for it gives access to the Fort at a point at which a good procession can be formed. On the other hand, the old approach was better for the purpose of defence, for, from the landing referred to above, the steps turned towards the east and led up to a gate built on the slope of the hill, so that the assailants were exposed to the missiles of the garrison at every stage of their progress. The old zigzag approach was built during the reign of Dilāwar Khān, and an inscription is carved on the inner gate of the approach, giving the date of the building.[2]

The old inner gate has an arched entrance, but to provide a place for the inscriptional tablet, the arch-head has been filled up with masonry and a lintel inserted near the springing-point (Plate XLVIII). The roof of the gateway was vaulted, and a portion of it is still intact. The passage below the roof extended to a length

[1] The inscription may be translated thus: 'During the government and administration of the servants of His Majesty, the shadow of God, Jalāl-ud-Dīn Muḥammad Akbar, the victorious King (May God protect his Kingdom!), this humble and insignificant (official), Ṭāhir Muḥammad Ḥusain 'Imād-ud-Dīn, son of Sulṭān 'Ali of Sabzwar, by divine grace succeeded in improving the main approach (to the Fort). Written in the month of Muḥarram in the year 1014 H. (May, A.D. 1605).'

[2] The inscription consists of five lines of Persian verse, and may be translated thus:

(1) 'The axis of Islamic faith, the chosen one of the nobility, the firmament of eminence and glory, the mine of benevolence.'

(2) 'The conqueror of the world, of youthful fortune and exalted

of 13 feet 6 inches, and was 10 feet 6 inches wide. The arch of the outer gate, which overlooked the valley, was loftier and more massive, and it has recently been properly conserved.

Akbar's Gate seems to have been built in a great hurry, for the masonry does not show careful workmanship. The square bastions on either side of the entrance have been much damaged by the overgrowth of trees; but under the systematic scheme for the conservation of the monuments of Mandū, wild trees and rank vegetation are now being cut away from the vicinity of the old buildings, the danger of their further decay being thus avoided for some considerable time.

Bhagwānīya Darwāzah

Facing the Nimar valley is another gate in the south wall of the Fort. It is called the Bhagwānīya Darwāzah, on account of the Bhagwānpūr village, which is situated in the valley at a distance of two to three miles. The gate can be approached on foot, either by walking along the wall of the Fort from Rūpmatī's Pavilions, or by proceeding along the foot-path which branches from the road to Bāz Bahādur's Palace near the outer walls of its fortification, and goes winding on for a distance of a mile and a quarter, first towards the east and then towards the south.

rank, powerful as fate, irresistible as destiny, the support of the universe.'

(3) 'The defence of the law of the prophet, the champion of the true faith, the cloud of bounty, the heaven of blessing, Dilāwar Khān.'

(4) 'He built a gate at Shādī Ābād, the like of which could not be traced even towards the region of Daulatabād.'

(5) 'Eight hundred and nine years had passed from the *Hijrat* when through the effort of the chosen one of the Lord the building was completed, 809 H. (A.D. 1406–7).'

The plan of the gateway begins with an outer entrance with lofty arches on the front and back and a vaulted roof above. The covered passage below is 10 feet 6 inches wide, while the span of the arches is 9 feet 6 inches. On proceeding beyond this entrance, the passage becomes a little wider, i.e. 13 feet 3 inches from side to side, and first goes towards the north and then towards the west until the inner entrance is reached. The passage between the two entrances, though open above, is defended on both sides by very massive walls.

The inner entrance is larger in dimensions than the outer, and the span of its arches is 11 feet 6 inches. The ceiling is vaulted, and for its support an arch has been set up across the passage, midway between the front and back arches of the entrance. The length of the covered passage is 22 feet 2 inches (its width is 13 feet), and on either side of it are built rooms for guards, which have been repeated in the upper storey of the building. The ceiling of the guard-rooms on the ground floor is pyramidal, with ribs at the joints.

Along the north wall of the entrance, steps have been built which lead first to the guard-rooms on the first floor and finally to the terrace above. The guard-rooms here are rectangular in plan (14 feet 6 inches by 7 feet 3 inches), and their ceilings are gabled.

The architecture of the Bhagwānīya Darwāzah is somewhat massive, but the proportion of its arches is well maintained.

Jahāngīrpūr Darwāzah

As the height of the hill in the eastern direction is not so considerable as on the other sides, the brink of the plateau has been defended by a massive wall, only one gate being built in this direction. This gate is styled the Jahāngīrpūr Darwāzah.

It is somewhat difficult to approach the gateway, for the foot-track which branches from the main road a little beyond the Sāgar Talāo is often lost in *nullahs* and thick forest, the abode of wild beasts.[1] The visitor is therefore advised to do the trek on a pony, and to take with him a *Bhīl* guide.

The plan of this gateway, like that of the others, consists of a double entrance with a winding passage intervening between them. Again, the outer entrance and its flanking walls are so built that they serve the purpose of a barbican for the inner entrance. The outer entrance is intact, but the roof of the inner one has fallen down and blocked the passage with debris. Along the north wall of the inner entrance, steps are built which lead to the terrace, where the remains of a kiosk may be seen. The carved pillars and lintels of the kiosk seem to have belonged originally to some Hindu building; but the architectural style of the Jahāngīrpūr Darwāzah is Moslem, resembling that of the Bhagwānīya and the Tārāpūr Darwāzahs.

Sāt sau Sīrhī

On referring to the Map, the reader will notice that the north-east side of the plateau has been cleft by a valley which stretches inward (west) right to the navel of the Fort. As the bed of this valley at certain points is not very deep, its mouth has, for the defence of the Fort, been closed by an embankment consisting of a

[1] The author's party, while returning from the gateway, lost their way in a *nullah*, and as night had set in, the experience of the fright and consternation of some of the party will ever remain a memorable feature of that excursion.

XLIX, JĀLĪ MAḤALL : INTERIOR

series of steps, hence the name 'Sāt sau Sīrhī', or 'Seven hundred steps'.

Rāmpol Darwāzah

This is situated at a short distance to the north-east of the Ashrafī Maḥall, and is perhaps one of the earliest gateways of Mandū. The piers of the outer arch, and the columns of the guard-rooms, built along the passage, exhibit Hindu workmanship, while the roof is of the Moslem style, being vaulted in the form of a barrel. It would appear that the original structure was in the trabeate style, but was afterwards rebuilt by the Musalmans, who utilized the masonry of the old building.

Inside the Fort, opposite the gateway, the remains of a mosque will be noticed. It consists of a double hall, divided into ten bays by the insertion of pillars. The ceiling of the inner five bays is composed of small domes, while that of the outer bays is pyramidal externally and in the form of a vault of six facets internally. The mosque has five arched openings towards the east, and the columns, instead of consisting of single shafts, are composed of several pieces, square in section and placed one above the other.

Lohānī Darwāzah

Corresponding to the Rāmpol Darwāzah, there is on the western brink of the plateau a gate styled the Lohānī Darwāzah. It is situated only a couple of furlongs to the west of Hoshang's Tomb (Map), and may easily be approached by a foot-track which ultimately leads to the lower end of the valley and to the small hamlets in the plains beyond.

The arch of the outer gate, which stood on the slope of the hill, has fallen down, but the piers are intact and may be seen. The remains of a guard-room are also to be noticed on the right side of the passage. The gate was built of red masonry.

About three-quarters of a furlong higher up are the ruins of another gate. The masonry of this building has carvings of the Hindu style, but the construction of the side walls discloses Musalman methods of building. It appears that, like the Rāmpol Darwāzah, this gate also was rebuilt by the Musalmans after their advent into Mandū.

While returning from the Lohānī Darwāzah, the visitor will notice in the wood to the right of the foot-path a shooting-box, a sight which may perhaps impart a thrill to his sporting instincts. Farther up he will pass by a mound which has on its top the remains of a tenth-century Hindu temple. Two piers marking the site of a doorway are still intact; they are elaborately carved, bearing figures of acrobats, animals, birds, and fabulous beings. Opposite this mound, on the other side of the track, there is another mound on which a monolithic column will be seen, rising 16 feet above the ground. The lower portion, to a height of 4 feet, is square, but above that it becomes octagonal, the width of each facet being nearly 10 inches. The top was originally crowned with a figure which has now disappeared.

At the back of the latter mound is the bed of a *nullah* in which the pieces of a carved *sikhara* (spire) and some sculptures are lying. Both the mounds would be worth excavating, for under the surface some inscriptions might be found which would throw light on the history of Mandū before the Musalman conquest.

Sāt Kothrī

To the lover of Hindu antiquities another site may appeal, which is called the Sāt Kothrī or the 'Seven

Cells'. They are situated on the slope of the rock outside the Fort of Mandū, and can be approached by turning off from the main road near the fourth furlong stone of the twenty-first mile, and walking a furlong and a half into the woods towards the west. There is in the rock a natural spring, around which the cells have been hewn out. Their dimensions are rather insignificant, and except a *linga* and a *yoni* there are no sculptures or carvings to be admired there. The natural scenery, however, as viewed from the cells, is superb; and the presence of the water and the beauty of the forest were perhaps the attractions which led some ascetic to excavate these chambers for meditation.

A little higher up than the cells, the visitor will notice the remains of a well, near which are lying the jamb of a richly-carved door and some sculptures. There seems to have been a Hindu temple in the vicinity at one time.

Jālī Maḥall (No. 2)

On returning to the road, the visitor will notice, on the opposite side to the last monument, a small mausoleum perched on a mound. It has no inscription stating the name of the noble whose last remains rest there, or mentioning the date of his demise. The style of the building, however, proves it to be a late sixteenth-century structure, when the Hindu and Musalman crafts had become welded together and the decorative detail of the former well fitted in with the architectural forms of the latter.

The mausoleum is built on a lofty platform which rises twenty-five steps higher than the landing where the foot-path leading from the road ends. The top of the platform, however, is not very spacious, measuring 52 feet square; while the mausoleum itself measures

19 feet on each side externally, and only 11 feet 10 inches square internally. The mausoleum has an arch in each of its four sides, the one towards the south being open, while the remaining three are closed by screens which are most delicately carved. There are two graves, the sarcophagi of which must once have been most beautiful; but they have been destroyed by vandals and the carved masonry taken away.

A pleasing feature of this tomb are the side projections of the piers of the arches, which, though architecturally devised to support the squinches, at the same time appear very graceful as a decorative theme (Plate XLIX). The carving of the pedestals of the piers also is extremely beautiful. The tomb is crowned by a shapely dome.

Conclusion

The visitor will now bid good-bye to this City of Joy (Shādīābād), and carry away his own impressions of the noble piles and delightful resorts; but in the effervescence of a joyous mood, or the depression of a pessimistic temper, he should not forget the feelings of the builders of these beautiful edifices which are so clearly expressed in the verse of Shāh Budāgh Khān on the Nīl Kanth Palace:[1]

> '*The whole of life well spent we deem*
> *In building thus, if o'er us gleam*
> *Some faintest hope that soul of grace*
> *Shall find repose within this place.*'

These are the feelings which have produced the greatest works of art in the world, and it is these feelings which have made the monuments of Mandū the brightest jewels of the architecture of India.

[1] *Supra*, p. 114.

INDEX

NOTE.—*The dates in parentheses following titles of monuments indicate the year or period of erection.*

'Abdul Karīm, engineer to Jahāngīr, probable builder of the Hāthī Pol Gate, 78.
'Abdu-l-Qādir, *see* Nāṣir-ud-Dīn.
Abū Sa'īd of Transoxiana, 17.
Abul Faḍl, quoted, 2 *n.* 2, 5, 11.
Adanson, M., French botanist, 2.
Adham Khān, 33; Mandū taken by, 31.
Agra, 28, 114; Hatyāpol Darwāzah at, 77–8.
Aḥmad Niẓām Shāh Baiḥrī of Ahmadnagar, 24.
Aḥmad Shāh Baihmanī of Gulbarga (1422–35), 10.
Ahmadnagar, 24.
'Ain-ul-Mulk, Mandū taken by (1305), 7.
Ajmer, 16.
Akbar, Emperor, 113 f.; annexes Malwa, 30–2; visits to Mandū, 33–4.
Akbar's Gate (1605), 117 f.; inscription on, 117 *n.* 1.
Akbarpur, palace at, 25; identification of, 25 *n.* 5.
'Ālamgīr I, *see* Aurangzeb.
'Ālamgīr Darwāzah, gateway (1668–9), 41–2; inscription on, 41 *n.* 1.
'Ala-ud-Dīn Khaljī, Sulṭān, 7.
Alp Khān, *see* Hoshang Shāh.
Amīr-ul-Mominīn Musta'īd Bi'llah Yūsuf of Egypt, 17.
Anand Rāo Puār, Deputy Governor of Malwa, 40.
'Anand-dew Rajpoot, building of Mandū ascribed to, 6.
Andherī Bāolī (the Dark Well), in Royal enclosure, 78; corridors in, 79.
Architecture, Mandū, three divisions of, 110 *n.* 2.
Āṣaf Khān, Gujarat general, 27.
Ashrafī Maḥall, *see* Madrasah.
Aurangzeb ('Ālamgīr I), Emperor, 41; inscription of, on Mandū gateway, 39.

Bahādur Shāh of Gujarat, Sulṭān (1526–37), 116; Mandū taken by, 27; defeat of, 28.
Bahlol Lodī, King of Delhi, 21.
Baobob (*Adansonia digitata*), tree, 2.
Bāradarī, a pavilion, 95 *n.* 1.
Barnes, Major E., quoted, 25 *n.* 5; visitors' rooms in Chhappan Maḥall named after, 111.
Barnes Kothī, visitors' rooms at Chhappan Maḥall, 111.
Bāz Bahādur (Malik Bāyazīd), Sulṭān of Malwa (1555–62), 25, 81, 91, 93; character of, 30; musical talents of, 31; defeat of, 32; buildings erected by, 32–3; gardens of, 36.
Bāz Bahādur's Palace (1508), 92–7; arched gateway, 93; court and pavilion, 94–5; the lower quadrangle, 96.
Beis, tribe, 6.
Bhagwānīya Darwāzah, 118–19; massive architecture of, 119.
Bhagwānpūr, village, 118.

Bhangī Darwāzah, 'Sweeper's Gateway' (? Hindu period), pillar-and-lintel style, 42–3.
Bidar, tomb of 'Alī Barīd at, 49 *n.* 1.
Biyana, state, 16.
Bundi, state, 16.
Burhanpur, 24.

Campbell, Sir J. M., quoted, 1 *n.* 2, 25 *n.* 5, 36.
Camping Ground, *see* Sāgar Talāo.
Caravan Sarāi, inn (? 1432), 86.
Chamkora diamond, 38 *n.* 2.
Champa Bāolī, well, in the Royal Palaces, 69, 78.
Champaner, fort, 27 f.
Chānd Khān, Prince, 27.
Chhappan Mahall (? 16th cent.), 110–11; best specimen of third period of Mandū architecture, 110; harmony of Hindu and Moslem style on exterior, 111; visitors' rooms, 111.
Chishtī Khān's Palace (? 16th cent.), 108–9; halls of the court, 109.
Chitor, 24.
Chitor, Queen of, 24.
'Classical' architecture of Mandū, 61.
Climate, 1–2.
Cordova, mosque at, 55 *n.*
Corryat, Thomas, 36; quoted, 79 *n.* 1.
Cousins, Henry, 105.

Dā'ī = wet-nurse, 86 *n.* 1.
Dā'ī Kā Mahall, monument (? 16th cent.), 88–9; the mosque, 89.
Dā'ī Kī Chhotī Baihan Kā Mahall, monument (? 16th cent.), 86–8; octagonal tomb, 87; Hindu masonry, 88.
Daryā Khān Lodi, official of Mahmūd II, 28.
Daryā Khān's Tomb (? 16th cent.), 28, 102–4; of transitional style, 102; domes and sepulchral hall, 103.
Dā'ud Khān of Khandesh, 24.
Daulat Khān, son of Shujā' Khān, 30.
Daulatabād, Chānd Mīnar at, 49 *n.* 1.
Deccan, 16, 113; Akbar's expeditions to, 33.
Delhi, 114; Mahmūd Khaljī's expedition against, 16 *n.* 5; Ustād Hāmid lane at, 48.
Delhi Darwāzah, gateway, 12, 43–4; inscription on, 44 *n.* 1.
Dhār, ancient capital of Malwa, 8 f., 40 f.
Dhār, Maharaja of, 82.
Dilāwar Khān Ghorī (Husain), Governor of Delhi (1401–5), 7; buildings erected by, 8–9.
Dilāwar Khān, Mosque of (1405), 44, 74–5; inscription on, 74 *n.* 1; the prayer-hall, 75.
Diya Bahādur, Governor of Mandū, 39.
Durgawatī, Rānī, Bāz Bahadūr defeated by, 30.

Echo Point, grove of trees, 89–90.

Fadl Ullah, physician of Mahmūd Khaljī, 19.
Fathabād, palace at, 18 *n.* 1.
Fauna, 2–3.
Fidwī Khān, Governor of Ranthambor, 19.
Finch, William, cited, 58 *n.*
Firishta, quoted, 6 ff., 10, 12 *n.* 1, 16 *n.* 5, 17 f., 19 *n.* 2, 20, 21 *n.* 5, 22, 25, 29 *n.* 2, 30.

Fīroz Tughluq, King of Delhi (1351–88), 8.
Flora, 2.
Fortifications described, 12 *n*. 1.

Gadā Shāh ('Beggar Master'), probable nickname of Medni Rā'i, 79 *n*. 3, 81.
Gadā Shāh's House (? 16th cent.), 28, 80–1; identification of paintings on, 81.
Gadā Shāh's Shop (?16th cent.), audience hall, 28; massive masonry of, 79–80.
Gārī Darwāzah, gateway, 43.
Ghaznī Khān, *see* Muḥammad Ghorī.
Ghiyāth-ud-Dīn, King of Malwa (1469–1500), 19; character of, 20–1; death of, 22; buildings erected by, 23.
Ghiyāth-ud-Dīn Balban of Delhi (1265–87), 7.
Great Mosque of Hoshang, *see* Jāmi' Masjid.
Gujarat, state, 16, 27.

Hāthī Maḥall (Elephant Palace) (? 16th cent.), 100–2; massive columns of, 101; the mosque, 101; hall with cistern, 102.
Hāthī Pol Gate (? 17th cent.), 77–8; effigies of elephants at, 77; notes on builder of, 77–8.
Hindolā Maḥall (15th cent.), 70–3; simplicity of architecture, 70–1; the main hall, 71–2; rectangular windows, 73; its replica at Warangal Fort, 73 *n*. 2.
Hindu style of architecture, Musalman influence on, 110 *n*. 2.
Holī, Hindu festival, 111 *n*. 1.
Hoshang Shāh (Alp Khān), King of Malwa (1405–32), 8; campaigns of, 9–10; expedition against the Raja of Jājnagar (1421), 10–11; character of, 11; buildings erected by, 12–13; death of, 13 f.
Hoshang, Mosque of, *see* Jāmi' Masjid.
Hoshang, Tomb of (15th cent.), 18, 45–50; domed porch, 45; door ornamentation, 46; casket sarcophagus, 47; conical domes, 48; inscription on, 48 *n*. 1; *Dharmasāla* colonnade and hall, 49–50; annual festival at, 50.
Hoshang II of Malwa, 26.
Hospital, founded by Maḥmūd Khaljī (1445), 19.
Humāyūn, Emperor, 30, 116; Mandū conquered by, 28.
Ḥusain, *see* Dilāwar Khān.

Ibrāhīm Shāh Sharqī of Jaunpūr (1400–40), 9.
'Imād-ud-Dīn Ḥusain, repaired Maḥmūd Khaljī's tomb, 59.
Indore, 3 f.
'Isā Khān, Governor of Malwa, 30.

Jahāngīr, Emperor, 105, 112; his banquets and functions at Mandū, 34–8; quoted, 1–2, 3, 6, 12 *n*. 1, 20 *n*. 3, 22, 23 *n*. 1, 34 *n*. 1.
Jahāngīrpūr Darwāzah, gateway (? 17th cent.), 119–20; of Moslem architecture, 120.
Jahāz Maḥall or Ship Palace (? 15th cent.), 23, 63–8; the Kapūr and Munja tanks, 63, 68; double hall, 64; pavilion, 64, 66; baths, 65, 67; view from terrace, 66.
Jai Sing, Raja, Governor of Malwa, 40.

Jājnagar (Orissa), 10.
Jājnagar, Raja of, Hoshang Shāh's expedition against (1421), 10–11.
Jālī Maḥall (No. 1), monument, Musalman carving on screens of, 90.
Jālī Maḥall (No. 2) (16th cent.), 123–4; carving of pedestals, 124.
Jāmi' Masjid, or Great Mosque of Hoshang (15th cent.), 12, 18, 50–6; inscription on, 51 *n.* 1; porch ornamentation, 52–3; colonnades, 53–5; Hindu ornamentation of pulpit, 55; exterior masonry, 56.
Jaunpur, state, 16.
Jayavarmadeva, copper-plate grant of, 6.

Kachwara, 19, 24.
Kairwan, mosque at, 52, 55 *n.*
Kākra Koh, gorge, 1, 41.
Kālpī, 9.
Kapūr Talāo (Camphor Tank), bordering the Jahāz Maḥall, 63, 68.
Khaljī dynasty, 34.
Khandesh, 24, 113.
Kherla, 9.
Khirkī Darwāzah, gateway, 43.
Khoosrow Purvees dynasty (590–628), 6.
Kotah, state, 16.
Kumbha, Rana of Mewar, 16, 18.

Lahore, 114.
La'l Maḥall (or Lāl Bungalow), 106–8; three divisions, 106; main court, 106–7; three-aisled colonnade of western division, 107; triple hall of eastern division, 108.
Lāt Masjid, pillar, at Dhār, 9.
Lohānī Darwāzah, gateway, 121–2.

Madrasah or Ashrafī Maḥall (? 15th cent.), 18, 57–8; arcades, 57; variety of arch spans, 58.
Mahābat Khān of Mandisor, 23.
Maḥmūd (I) Khaljī, King of Malwa (1436–69), 2, 13, 24; murders Muḥammad Ghorī, 14–15; conquests of, 16; character of, 17; buildings erected by, 18–19; death of, 19.
Maḥmūd Khaljī, Tomb of (15th cent.), 34, 59–61; inscription on, 59 *n.* 1; Persian carving and calligraphy, 60; instability of structure, 61. *See also* Tower of Victory.
Maḥmūd II, Sulṭān of Malwa (1510–26), 25; wars of, 26–7; death of, 27; buildings erected by, 28.
Maḥmūd Tughluq of Delhi, Sulṭān, 8.
Mainas, talking birds, 17.
Malcolm, Sir John, 18 *n.* 1; quoted, 40.
Malhar Rāo Holkar, Malwa invaded by, 39.
Malik Bāyazīd, *see* Bāz Bahādur.
Malik Maḥmūd Khān, *see* Maḥmūd (I) Khaljī.
Malik Mughīth, minister of Hoshang, 13, 15.
Malik Mughīth, Mosque of (1432), 14, 82–6; inscription on, 82 *n.* 1; hybrid style of architecture, 83; arched corridor, 83; arches of porch, 84; colonnades—carving of ceiling, 84–5; domes, 85.
Mallū Khān, *see* Qādir Shāh.

Malwa, Muḥammadan conquest of (13th cent.), 7; independence of (1401), 7 ff.; struggles with Gujarat, 9, 16, 26; annexation to Gujarat (1526), 27; conquered by Humāyūn (1534), 28; by Sher Shāh (1536), 29; surrendered to Akbar (1562), 32; Maratha conquest of (1732), 39–40.
Mandisor, state, 16; siege of, 15.
Maratha invasions of Malwa, 39–40.
Marshall, Sir John, 60.
'Medieval' architecture of Mandū, 61.
Mednī Rā'i, rebel minister of Maḥmūd II, 26; buildings erected by, 28; his association with Gadā Shāh's Shop and House, 28, 79 *n*. 3, 81.
Mewar, province, 16.
Mhow, 3 f.
Mīrān Mubārak Khān of Khandesh, 31, 33.
Mubārak, Syed, King of Delhi, 16 *n*. 5.
Muḥammad, Sulṭān of Delhi, 8.
Muḥammad, Syed, King of Delhi, 16 *n*. 5.
Muḥammad II (Sāḥib Khān) of Malwa, 26.
Muḥammad 'Abbāsī, Caliph of Egypt, 17.
Muḥammad Beg Khān, 'Ālamgīr Darwāzah erected by, 41 *n*. 1.
Muḥammad Ghorī (Ghaznī Khān), King of Malwa (1432–6), 13; murder of, 14.
Muḥammad Husain, agent of Akbar, 117.
Muḥammad Khān, Pīr, Governor of Malwa, 31.
Muḥammad Khān Bangash, Governor of Mandū, 40.
Muḥammad Shāh, King of Delhi (1389–94), 7.
Munja, Paramara king, 6 *n*. 6.
Munja Talāo, tank, 6 *n*. 6, 63 f., 68 ff.
Murād, Prince, son of Akbar, Governor of Malwa (1592), 33.
Musalman conquest, 7; influence on Hindu architecture, 110 *n*. 2.
Muṣṭafa Khān, son of Shujā' Khān, 30.
Muẓaffar Shāh I of Gujarat, 10.
Muẓaffar Shāh II of Gujarat, 26; banquet given to, 26 *n*. 7.

Nahār Jharokā or Tiger Balcony (? 17th cent.), 75–6; halls, 76.
Nalcha, 18 *n*. 1, 41.
Narbada, river, 5, 99 f., 79 *n*. 1.
Nāṣir-ud-Dīn, Sulṭān ('Abdu-l-Qādir), King of Malwa (1500–10), 19, 93; Ghiyāth-ud-Dīn poisoned by, 22; wars of, 23–4; character of, 24–5; death of, 25; buildings erected by, 25.
Nīl Kanth (Blue Throat) Palace (? 16th cent.), 34, 111–14; court and cistern, 112; Akbar's inscriptions, 113 *n*. 1; Mughal features of, 114.
Nimar, district and valley, 41, 105, 118.
Niẓām-ud-Dīn, quoted, 31.
Nūr Jahān Begam, wife of Jahāngīr, 36, 38 *n*. 2; palace of, 35.
Nuṣrat Khān, Governor of Malwa, 10.

Palaces, Royal, 68 ff.
Paramara dynasty (8th–13th cent.), 6.

Peshwa Bājī Rāo, Maratha Governor of Malwa (1734), 40.
Pillars, Mandū style of, 69–70.
Pīr Ghaib, the 'invisible saint', grave at Songarh, 116.
Pol=gateway, 56 *n.* 1.

Qādir Shāh (Mallū Khān), King of Malwa (1536–42), 28–9.
Qarauli, state, 16.

Rai Mahlak Deo of Malwa, slain at Mandū (1305), 7.
Raja Jai Sing Deva, legend of, 5–6.
Rāmpol Darwāzah, Hindu and Moslem style, 121.
Ranthambor, state, 16, 21.
Rīwā Kund, reservoir (16th cent.), 36, 105; legend of, 32 *n.* 3; sanctity of waters, 91; halls, 92.
Roe, Sir Thomas, 34, 36, 79; location of his residence at Mandū, 105–6.
Routes to Mandū, 3–4.
Royal enclosure, 105; triple gateway of (? 16th cent.), 61 (*see also* Hāthī Pol Gate); medieval style of buildings in, 61. For buildings in, *see* pp. 61–78.
Rūpmatī, wife of Bāz Bahādur, 30 f., 33, 81, 91, 93.
Rūpmatī's Pavilions (? 15th cent.), 97–100, 105; the original hall, 97–8; inscription on, 98; basement, 98–9; pavilions, 99–100; sunset view from, 100.

Sāgar Talāo ('Sea Tank') or Camping Ground, pleasure resort, 81–2, 105.
Sāgarī Tank and Garden, 88.
Ṣāḥib Khān, *see* Muḥammad II of Malwa.
Salīm Shāh, Sulṭān of Delhi, 29.
Samarqand, state, 17.
Sarangpur, 31.
Sāt Kothrī, or 'Seven Cells', 122–3.
Sāt sau Sīrhī, or 'Seven hundred steps', 120–1.
Sayyid Mubārak Shāh, King of Delhi (1421–33), 9.
Shab-i-Barāt, Mughal festival, 34 f.
Shādīābād, 'City of Joy' = Mandū, 9, 124.
Shāh, derivation of term, 28 *n.* 1.
Shāh Budāgh Khān, Governor of Mandū (1568), 34; quoted, 124.
Shāhjahān, Emperor, visits to Mandū, 38–9; wealth of, 38 *n.* 2; his respect for Mandū architecture, 48.
Shams-ud-Dīn Iltutmish, Ujjain conquered by, 7.
Sher Khān, Governor of Chanderi, 23.
Sher Shāh, Emperor, 23; Malwa invaded by, 29 and *n.* 2.
Shihāb-ud-Dīn, Prince, son of Nāṣir-ud-Dīn, 25 f.
Ship Palace, *see* Jahāz Maḥall.
Shiraz, state, 17.
Shitāb Khān, Governor of Warangal, Hall of Justice of, a replica of the Hindolā Maḥall, 73 *n.* 2.
Shujā' Khān, Governor of Malwa (1545–54), 29–30.
Shuja't Khān, son of Ghiyāth-ud-Dīn, 22.
Shujāwalpūr, 30 *n.* 2.
Sikandar Khān of Erich, 23.
Sikandar Lodī of Delhi, Sulṭān, 26.

Situation, 1.
Siva, Hindu deity, 111.
Songarh, 1, 28, 115–16; fortifications and gateway, 115; grave of Pīr Ghaib at, 116.

Tārāpūr, village, 116.
Tārāpūr Gate (15th cent.), 8, 34, 116–18; approach defences, 117; arched entrance, 117–18. *See also* Akbar's Gate.
Ṭawelī Maḥall, 'stables mansion', 61–3; dimensions of the three floors, 62–3.
Temple, Hindu (10th cent.), near the Lohānī Darwāzah, 122.
Terry, Rev. Edward, 36, 78, 106.
Tīmūr Lang, invasion of India (1398), 7 f.
Tīrla, 40.
Tomb north of Daryā Khān's Mausoleum, 104–6; gallery and mosque, 104; probable site of Roe's residence, 105–6.
Tower of Victory, Maḥmūd Khaljī's (15th cent.), 58–9.
Trīpolīya Gate, trap masonry of, 56–7.

Udi Singh, Rana of Mewar, 32.
Ujālā Bāolī (the Bright Well), in Royal enclosure, corridors in, 78–9.
Ujjain, 7.
'Urs, religious assembly, 11.
Ustād Ḥāmid, architect of Shāhjahān, 48 and *n.* 1.

Vindhyan Range, 1.

Warangal Fort, Hall of Justice of Shitāb Khān at, 73 *n.* 2.
Water Pavilion, in the Royal Palaces, 70.